The *Missouri* *Review*

Volume XXII Number 1   1999

University of Missouri—Columbia

The Missouri Review is published by the College of Arts & Science of the University of Missouri-Columbia, with private contributions and assistance from the Missouri Arts Council and the National Endowment for the Arts.

The editors invite submissions of poetry, fiction and essays of a general literary interest with a distinctly contemporary orientation. Manuscripts will not be returned unless accompanied by a stamped, self-addressed envelope. Please address all correspondence to The Editors, *The Missouri Review*, 1507 Hillcrest Hall, University of Missouri, Columbia, Missouri, 65211.

SUBSCRIPTIONS
1 year (3 issues), $19.00
2 years (6 issues), $35.00
3 years (9 issues), $45.00

Copyright © 1999 by The Curators of the University of Missouri
ISSN 0191 1961   **ISBN** 1-879758-25-3
Printed by Thomson-Shore   Distributed by Ingram Periodicals

The Missouri Review

CONTENTS — 1999

POETRY (continued)

ESSAYS

BOOK REVIEWS

"You speak Gobbledygook! Excellent!"

Foreword

Writers have won *The Missouri Review* Editors' Prize at different stages in their writing lives, but we have noticed that historically they tend to be in early career. We've always thought of "career" as independent of age, since some of our best first or early-career pieces are written by authors who are not young. One of the things I enjoy about working on the magazine is finding out about the identities of the writers we publish. They often surprise you: a voice that is terribly mature may come from a young writer, or one that is wayward and agile may be from someone middle-aged or older. A white writer can sound black. A woman can sound like a man. The voice in one story we took was so believably boylike that I was sure we were accepting a piece from a brilliant schoolchild, only to discover he was a sophisticated adult who wrote in all kinds of voices. To me, it's a cheery thing, this sharing of voices, this ventriloquism, this ability to imagine oneself in the shoes of another. A voice "in the groove," wholly convincing—this is one of the things I live for as a reader.

Something else about the contest I noticed this year was how many submissions we received from people working in the publishing industry, all happily making use of their magazine's or publishing house's envelopes. Multinational publishing conglomerates, beware: the extremely well-educated young people whom you are paying $21,000 a year to slave away at your profit centers are stealing envelopes to enter literary contests. (Literary? What's literary? Find out who's stealing those *New Yorker* 9" X 12" envelopes!)

The young and starving on the coasts, the sixty-somethings, the middle-aged and yearning, the writing program kids, a few big names—all were among the entrants this year, and all were treated equally. Yes, it sells magazines to have well-known writers plastered on the cover, but we have also noticed that when literary magazines publish only well-known writers, it is a very good bet that those magazines are being poorly edited. They are publishing advertisable names rather than content and thus have forfeited their principal advantage as noncommercial magazines.

I get testy about well-funded nonprofit organizations that give prizes and awards only to the already severely bemedaled "safe" writers—the second lieutenants of literature—who stagger from one writers' conference to the next. Although this isn't the case with all of the nonprofits, there are some egregious examples—organizations run by time-servers who either have no confidence in their opinions or perhaps don't have any opinions of their own.

We relish discovery. We are delighted when agents and publishers call, as they do after every issue, asking how to get in touch with our writers. Yes, we say, love to give you their addresses. That's what we're here for.

The content of this issue, though—I just don't know. We have tried to put the best face on things and make it sound highbrow, or at least neutral-brow, by calling it "altered states," but as far as I'm concerned it might as well be called the WEIRD issue or the STRANGE TALES issue. "Altered states" is a little bogus, come to think of it, given the fact that the altering of states is a bit like $E=mc^2$ of literature. You can pretty much count on it: the story doesn't start until a change occurs; the poem is made possible when something is perceived anew.

But there is some peculiar stuff in these pages—ghosts, bizarre life changes, shadowy mysteries. Emily Pease's Editors' Prize–winning story, "Tad Lincoln's Ladder of Dreams," is narrated by a ghost, the dead younger son of President and Mrs. Lincoln—a fitting voice for the scary tale of a family stalked by death. As well as anything I've read about the subject, Pease's story offers insights into the martyrdom of the Lincolns to illness, war, murder, and madness.

Stephanie Rosenfeld and Michael Byers are two pokerfaced comic writers. In Rosenfeld's "Grasp Special Comb" a woman separated from her husband finds the pieces of her life "flying irretrievably in different directions" when her daughter brings home lice. Byers' deadpan "The Largest Room" depicts a designer of NASA steering mechanisms who begins to suffer physical symptoms so curious and disturbing that they threaten to launch him into his own kind of orbit.

Two of our stories concern outright mysteries. In William Richardson's "The Spring House," an interested outsider tries to puzzle out the story of an outcast couple from an Amish community. Steve Adams' story, "The Chosen," features an insurance adjustor faced with explaining an accident that completely defies reason.

All four poets in this issue are travelers in time and space. In his poems about Oedipus and Penelope in the 1990s—divorced and worrying about Telemachos—Larry Levis Poetry Prize winner Jeffrey Levine refurbishes the ideas of heroism and fidelity. Adrie Kusserow writes of a young woman hungry for spiritual change, a haunted seeker at faraway monasteries. Susan Terris turns the commonplace into the remarkable by reconfiguring, through a middle-aged woman's eyes, the summer-camp world of girlhood sexuality. Morri Creech commingles the landscape of his childhood farm with delirious visions of the Old Testament.

Editors' Prize–winning essay "Hep-Lock," by Adria Bernardi, depicts what it is like to be transformed almost overnight from a state of robust health to one of life-threatening illness. Repeat *Missouri Review* writer Carl Schiffman's altered state is from work to retirement, and it allows him to write with candor and passion about a lifetime of experience as a white administrator and fundraiser for civil rights. In the essay, he bluntly addresses the incompetence of former fellow bureaucrats, as well as continued inequalities of education and opportunity for blacks. Melanie Hammer writes about an extreme case of shyness and introversion, and an attempt to break out of it.

One of the big changes in novelist Ernest Gaines' career was from pre- to post-Oprah. Yet for the notably down-to-earth Gaines, whose whole life has been devoted to writing, the magic wand of the queen of bookselling didn't make all that much difference. It didn't really alter his state.

There you have it. Bogus again. We'll try to do better next time.

SM

"Your 'Ode To A Prospect' was the most
original sales letter I've ever received."

"Now for the busy signal torture!"

THE LARGEST ROOM/*Michael Byers*

IT WAS MARCH, SOMETIME late in the afternoon on a Wednesday, and the spring wind blew gusts of rain theatrically against Mark Horton's single, unopenable window, which gave only a wan light to his cramped and cluttered office, casting a gray veil over the computer, the stacks of paper, the empty bottles of water, the thin brown carpet of this very small room where he'd been working, programming, for an untold number of days in a row. Actually he couldn't remember the last time he'd bothered with a day off; he'd been writing and figuring and then jogging at all hours, too, when he felt the need, running on the concrete path across the mud flats behind the engineering building, past the oily river as it went sliding through its greasy banks, then into the gym shower quickly and to his desk again, where he kept on, sometimes sleeping here, sometimes driving home not knowing for sure whether it was dawn or dusk. It was a life he'd never imagined for himself, but he'd come to enjoy it, the desperate last-days feel of it, and everyone knew this latest bad spell was temporary, really, another week or so and everyone could go back to normal, take a weekend off even. The rain increased now, the bare tree outside the window scrabbled its long black branches, and Mark went on typing, heedless.

Then, all at once, without warning, and as the rain continued its maniacal flailing, Mark Horton's hands went numb. He batted them together but felt nothing. He was alarmed. He turned his wrists, examining one side of his hands, then the other, two squarish and peculiar fish. He hadn't really looked at them recently, he thought, their dry and puckery knuckles, the chewed-down cuticles spotted here and there with dried blood, the blond hairs all waving one way, like grass on the beach, as if they, too, like everything else, were subject to the wind.

He walked next door to Alistair McCauley's office and pushed the door aside with his shoulder. "My hands," he said, "I've lost the feeling in my hands."

Alistair McCauley, a homeopath in his spare time, not yet forty but in Mark's eyes an oldish man who drank green tea instead of coffee, was bent eagerly into his computer, as though it were feeding him, his long, rapier-like nose following white text as it scrolled up the screen. McCauley paid him no attention.

"My hands just went numb," Mark said.

McCauley said, "What?"

"My hands." Mark flapped them.

"Repetitive motion does that sometimes." McCauley dug into a desk drawer and took out a wrist brace. "Numbness and pain."

"No," Mark said. "Not pain. Just nothing." He flapped them again at the ends of his arms, forcing himself to look at them. "Just numbness."

McCauley stood up and took Mark's hands in his own. McCauley's long, bony nose was pitted with scars, but his teeth, behind narrow lips, shone a brilliant, almost artificial white and were perfectly even, like cigarettes in a pack. "No feeling?" He pinched one fleshy thumb, then the other. "No nothing?"

"No."

McCauley took a pen from his pocket and began poking Mark's palms. Little blue dots appeared here and there. "Nothing?"

"No. It just happened. Just suddenly."

"Well, I don't know what that is. That's not like carpal tunnel."

"No." His hands hung heavily, loosely, from his wrists, as though attached with string.

McCauley regarded him with some seriousness. "Could be a brain tumor, that sudden loss of sensation." He rubbed a dirty finger under his nose. "Though I doubt it. Dizziness? Double vision? Nausea?"

"No."

"I can look it up when I get home. Maybe you're just going crazy. Psychosomatosis. Been under any unusual stress lately? Any major changes in your life situation? Death? Divorce? Loss of a job?"

"I have to go home," Mark said.

"Oh, lucky man." McCauley shuffled back to his computer. "Take notes and tell me what it's like."

Mark went back to his office, maneuvered himself into his overcoat, and jumped up and down to be sure his keys were in his pocket. He turned off his computer with the side of his wrist and made his way out through the long, carpeted hallways. Outside, though it took him a long time to separate his car key from the rest of his keys, and he needed a minute or so to work the key into the ignition, and it was difficult to start the car, driving itself wasn't particularly hard; on the concrete-walled freeway he drove home in the slow lane, and the high rubber hum of his tires echoed back to him as he steered with his wrists. He even managed to use his turn signal and, pulling into the garage, found himself proud of his dexterity. This wouldn't be so bad, he thought.

Mark Horton designed steering programs for the space shuttle, one of twenty men to do so, and had been at it now for five years, coming on just before the Challenger crash and working—doggedly, really—through those months when they did nothing but plan, and plan, trade conjecture back and forth, and wait for everything to come back to normal. The trauma had been absolute, and many men had quit, taking jobs with Boeing next door, or doing something else entirely. As for Mark, he'd saved the newspapers that day and taped the newscasts, and out of some perversion or sentiment he kept the paper coffee cup he'd been drinking from that morning, the curled lip of the cup bitten flat and the rim marked here and there with the curves of his old brown mouthprints. He kept it in the back of a drawer, at work, and was always more or less aware of it.

He was able to make his way inside his building, but his mail, alluring in its metal box, was beyond him, the key too small to maneuver, and he went off to the elevator. He lived in one of the city's older apartment buildings, brick and squat, built probably in the 1920s, the moldings in the hallways simple but pleasant to look at, the large, sloping bathtub suggesting to him an era, now lost utterly, of decadence and easily available sex. From his front windows he could see down the tilted hillside to Lake Union, and at night the lake was a smooth piece of black emptiness in the spangled cityscape. Seaplanes took off and landed, and when they coasted in under no power, their propellers feathered the air with a gentle avian sound that Mark had come to associate with his elegant and underused apartment.

When he opened the front door, maneuvering his keys in the lock with his wrists, his telephone was ringing on the coffee table. He dropped his keys and, still in his raincoat, lifted the receiver off its hook with the insides of his forearms. Then he laid the receiver on the coffee table and knelt to speak into it, tipping his head so he could hear, distantly, the noises from the earpiece. It was Anita, who was more or less his girlfriend.

"Anita," he said loudly, "my hands went numb." He began shrugging off his raincoat but stopped, deciding it would take him too far from the telephone.

"Well, there's a dead raccoon in my yard. It's up in a tree and I can't get it down. I think someone threw it up there. It's those kids."

"I can't even make a cup of coffee."

"Bullshit," she said.

"It's true. My hands are numb."

"You're so full of it."

"I'm not," he said. "It just happened. I'm sitting here kneeling and talking to you with the phone on the coffee table."

"Just come help. You don't have to really do anything."

From his peculiar angle he looked around at the bare walls of his apartment, wondering why he'd never hung anything up. The place seemed sleazy, provisional. He had never noticed it before, but it was true. "You don't understand," he said.

"Please. I'll make you some tea. I have this new tea."

He felt his hands tingling and looked at them suspiciously. He would go; of course he would go.

He and Anita had been sleeping together off and on for just over a year. Now, in the second year of what she called their relationship, he didn't like her much anymore; she was unspectacular in bed and given to moaning, which he didn't like, and really, if he were to be honest about it, she was not very bright. She'd once told him that as a child she'd wanted to be an astronaut, which made Mark dislike her even more, her frizzy hair, oversized glasses, and big hips all making her seem the most earthbound of people.

Her bathroom was always cluttered with balms and lotions; they gave a greasy feel to her skin, which was clammy to begin with. She was an accountant in Foreign Sales and spoke fluent Arabic, but only because her grandfather had been Lebanese, and not, Mark often reminded himself, because she'd actually put any effort into it. He'd met her a year ago at a company picnic, to which he'd gone reluctantly; she'd been standing at the edge of the crowd with two pieces of corn on her paper plate. He'd been lonely, and he slept with her, and it was fine for a few weeks. Now he regretted it, but he hadn't the heart, or maybe the courage (yes, it *was* courage, he thought, of course it was, no getting around it), to get rid of her.

On the way to Anita's house he began to feel the steering wheel under his hands, faintly, like an echo of real feeling, and he was heartened; it couldn't be anything serious, he thought—just one of those things. Happily, he ran his hands over the cloth seats of his car.

Anita was in the back yard with a metal rake, looking up into the splayed branches of her cherry tree, where a dark, furry clump sat, obviously dead, obviously a raccoon. Anita, who worked flextime at Boeing, had on red gym shorts and a green tank top, and her plastic glasses were halfway down her nose. "Look at that," she said fiercely. "The nerve."

Still in his trenchcoat, he looked. "It could have died up there," he said. "Raccoons have heart attacks."

"No. Somebody threw it." She glanced at him. "How're your hands?"

"Better." The raccoon's fur ruffled in the wind. "You call Animal Control?"

"They charge money." She was peering at the side of his face now, rather too intently. "You look a little funny," she said. "You look a little insane."

"Yeah, well." He pulled his hands out of his pockets and slapped them together, felt a faint sting. "They're almost back." He took the rake without much difficulty. He was taller than Anita, had a longer reach, and he poked at the raccoon until it came thumping down out of the tree. In the grass it looked like a cartoon, with large brown eyes and pointy teeth. She said, "Fucking kids," gave him a shovel, and held open a plastic bag. The raccoon slid into the bag, surprisingly light for its size, and Anita spun the bag closed and tied it.

Mark picked up the lid of the trash can with no problem at all. "Okay," he said, relieved. "I think they're back."

"Come on inside."

Anita took him inside and gave him a cup of green, sickish tea, the same sort that McCauley drank. They sat together on the sofa and listened to the radio for half an hour, kissing without much progress, and despite himself Mark began to feel some real affection for Anita, with her friendly, heavy shoulders against his. But then Mark stood up, put his cup on the coffee table, and said good-bye. When he was rational, which was not all the time, he felt an alternating contempt and pity for Anita, and both made him feel guilty, but not so much that he wanted to do something about it. He drove home slowly, stopping at yellow lights, taking his time, and that night he slept soundly, like a child, in his white, undecorated room.

Mark Horton was afraid of hospitals and doctors, but the next morning—it was sunny, and the mountains were out in both directions—he drove himself to his clinic, a little gray building next to a laundromat. Inside, he announced himself to the receptionist, a pale woman with green eyeshadow, then sat down and read an article about lead poisoning. He gazed at the illustrations, men and women in goutish contortions of abdominal agony. It was not the sort of thing he would have put in his waiting room.

In the corner chair, a woman in an orange parka sat with her palms pressed tightly over her eyes, as though she were holding them in; every so often she took the hands away and looked at him, blinking, then covered her eyes again.

"Trouble with your vision?"

"No shit," she said. "Bastard."

At last the nurse called him in and brought him to an examining room. She was young and black-haired, and to Mark's eyes she was a little slatternly, her mouth wide and inviting, and though she said nothing in particular he sensed a willingness on her part. He described his symptoms, said that he had been working a good deal lately, and mentioned, offhand, the sort of work he did, but she seemed unimpressed. "Sudden numbness," she said, writing it down. When the doctor, Dr. Eich, possibly German or Dutch, but definitely foreign, came with her pursed little mouth and tiny gold-rimmed glasses, she banged on his knees with a hammer. She poked the backs of his hands with a very small electronic needle, which hummed, and she shone her flashlight into his eyes. "Okay," she said finally. "I want to do a scan of your head."

"My head?"

"Your brain, I mean. It's probably carpal tunnel and that's all there is to it, but it's a strange manifestation and so just to be on the safe side . . ." She snapped her flashlight off and slid it back into her deep white pocket. "Don't worry," she said. She picked up the phone. After, he was instructed to drive immediately to the hospital, where they would be expecting him.

"Now, you mean?"

"Yes, now. You want to put this off? No."

Out in the waiting room, the woman in the orange parka had picked up and was reading his magazine, quite without difficulty, it seemed. As he passed the woman, Mark kicked her chair squarely and with obvious intention, his sneakered toe grazing her bare calf. Then he walked quickly on his way, got into his car, and drove to work.

McCauley was there, lumped in his gray sweatshirt. "The kid's back," he said, looking him up and down. "How's the hands?"

"Okay. It went away."

"Yeah, well, I know what it is now. I was reading up on it last night. That's Randolf-Doyle syndrome, I'd bet my ass on it. Turn around."

Mark turned around.

"Randolf-Doyle is when you add chronic nerve inflammation to a peculiarly shaped spine and you get sudden and sporadic numbness, particularly at periods of high stress. Take off your shirt."

Mark peeled off his T-shirt. His armpits smelled strange, like a burnt match.

"And sulfuric perspiration, Jesus." McCauley ran a finger down Mark's spine, counting the vertebrae, and Mark shivered. "That's Bittmenn's complex, the sulfur."

"What's that?"

"Excessive potassium intake coupled with loose bowels. How's your shitting?"

"Fine."

"Well," McCauley said, "your spine is peculiar."

"It is?"

"It's got a jog in it, here." He poked Mark between the shoulder blades.

"Really?" Mark craned around to look but couldn't see anything. "No one's ever said that before."

"Maybe nobody ever looked."

Mark put his shirt back on.

McCauley sat on his desk, lifted one tennis shoe into the air. "Now," he said, "with the Randolf-Doyle I can't do all that much for you. I mean, I can give you a magnesium dose for the inflammation, but the spine is obviously beyond me. The Bittmenn's is easy, that's just a cyanidium dose maybe twice a day."

Mark said, "Cyanidium?"

"I'm a homeopath. Believe me, I know what I'm doing."

"I know what you are."

McCauley went to his desk and took out a black leather case. Inside were little vials of identical white pills. "This," he said, "is my pharmacopoeia." He dropped pills into two white envelopes and labeled them, wrote out the dosages.

"Jeez, cyanidium."

"It's a tiny little dose." McCauley reached into the envelope and took a pill, swallowed it. "See? It can't hurt you."

"Still."

"Trust me," he said. "I've been doing this for years."

Around eleven that night Mark drove home and turned on the television news. A water main had burst downtown, and buses sloshed through the streets. In the Kingdome, men and women threw paper airplanes from the third level, trying to win a car. Two old women, sisters, separated for forty years, were reunited in Sea-Tac.

His hands weren't bothering him, but he was wary.

He took McCauley's two envelopes from his jeans pocket and smoothed them on his knee. Magnesium, one said, five pills a day, under the tongue until dissolved. Cyanidium, the other said, one pill a day, under the tongue until dissolved. The pills were tiny, like ball bearings, and indistinguishable from one another: white and powdery. He took one of each and set them under the ligament of his tongue; they had a sweetish taste. He sat and watched the news until they were gone. They left a pasty feel in his mouth that he washed out with root beer.

In the middle of the night he woke in his undecorated bedroom with the sensation that things were on the verge of turning inside out. The walls were about to unzip themselves and turn their unpainted sides outward; the lightbulb in his lamp wanted to peel itself open like a pear; his hands wanted to come off like gloves. He sat up cautiously and looked around the darkened room. Nothing had changed. Light from the street slanted through the window onto the floor. A car passed outside, playing music, then went on. In his mind the car, too, wanted to turn inside out. So did the driver and the street. The city, everything.

Carefully, so as not to disturb anything, Mark Horton dressed and went slowly downstairs. It was three in the morning, and the city was quiet. The street in front of his apartment was empty except of parked cars. Overhead the clouds glowed orange and brown. He sat down on the steps of the building. It had to be the pills, he thought. Or if he had a brain tumor, it was that. One or the other. He sat there for another hour. Slowly the feeling subsided, and eventually it faded away entirely. He sat for another ten minutes, until the world was full again of familiar surfaces; then he went back to bed.

The next morning he woke to the phone ringing. It was Dr. Eich, asking why he hadn't gone to the hospital.

"I felt fine," he said, sitting up in bed. Everything was normal again. Sunlight lay in panes over the floor.

"That's not the point," she said. "You need your brain examined. I'll make another call. Okay? You go this time, right?"

"Sure," Mark said. He wasn't sure of anything. "I'll go."

"Maybe Friday is good for you. A week from today."

"Friday's fine."

"Okay," the doctor said, and gave him a time.

"That's fine."

The doctor cleared her throat. "You be good, now," she said. "Don't get me in trouble."

McCauley said, "I don't know what that is, things turning inside out. I've never heard of it."

"They didn't turn, exactly. They *almost* turned. Like everything *wanted* to turn. Like things had a will."

"Oh," McCauley sighed. "I don't know. Maybe Mannstein's. But it's not classic Mannstein's. That's when you think everything's about to lift off from the earth." He closed his kit. "I don't have anything for that."

"You don't feel it when you take that stuff?"

McCauley shrugged. "I'm telling you. They're harmless." He opened his kit again, took out two pills, and put them under his tongue.

"Okay," Mark said. His alarm returned. "So maybe I have a brain tumor."

"Doubtful. In fact, almost impossible. Listen. I can give you the sort of second-tier doses. They're different medicines."

"Why don't we do that."

"Good man," McCauley said, and began sifting out pills again. "Same deal with these."

Mark took the pills and went next door to work. His office now looked homey and welcoming, and he turned on his computer with some flair. This, he thought, was normal life. He let the pills disappear under his tongue, and then he waited, but for a long while nothing happened.

Halfway through the day, he began to sense something. There was, he felt, a great empty space growing inside him: a cavern somewhere between his heart and his groin, expanding and expanding. He touched his gut experimentally; nothing felt unusual from the outside. He stood up and walked around the office, carrying the space with him. He pulled up his shirt and tapped his fingers on his belly.

He went next door.

"Okay," he said, describing it, "explain that one."

McCauley rolled his head on his neck and thought for a moment. "Maybe gas."

"It's those medicines."

"Yeah," McCauley said. "Either it is or it isn't."

"I don't mind this one so much." There were miles and miles of space inside him; it would take a day to walk all the way from one side of him to the other. "It's sort of strange, but it's not bad, exactly."

"Okay," McCauley said, typing. "If it suits you, it suits me."

The next day, and the next, he continued the dosage—two artinium a day, three floxisporum—and the feeling stayed about the same. At night, in his apartment, he walked the space from room to room, feeling it move obediently along inside him. He maneuvered himself carefully through doorways, though he knew he was nowhere near as large as he felt; he went to work as he always did and stayed very late, but he stopped running because running felt strange to him. It was a curiosity, the whole thing was. When he lay down the space seemed to lie down, too, turning on an axis, and when he slept, he slept on his back and didn't turn over. He began to waddle a little, as a pregnant woman would, though he was no fatter than he ever had been.

After two days of this, Dr. Eich called him again, at work. "Just reminding you," she said, "about Friday." It was Monday.

"I remember." He palmed his belly.

"Anything new?"

"Well," he said, "in a way." He explained as best he could. "It doesn't hurt. In fact it feels sort of interesting."

"You're not on any drugs?"

He gave her the names of the pills.

"No, that's nothing. That won't do anything to you." He could hear her smacking her lips. "You're an interesting case, Mr. Horton."

"Thank you."

"I wonder if what you're describing is really organic. You're under some stress, I imagine?"

"Some," he said. "But nothing unusual. We're working very hard."

"Perhaps," she said, "it is time to see a mental health professional."

"Anything you want." He was filled with oceanic calm. "Give me a name."

"Go see Dr. Boxer. He's a good one. Not a crackpot, like some of them. Maybe we do a double-dip Friday for you."

"Okay," he said. "I'm sorry, by the way, about the other day."

"Yeah. He'll charge *me*, you know, so don't skip out."

That night he drove unannounced to Anita's house. She came to the door in her sweats. "Anita," he said. He hadn't spoken to her since the day of his hands.

"Oh, guess what," she said, looking past him into the yard. "I caught the kids. Came home this afternoon and they were out there skulking around. I showed up and they just disappeared. But I nailed them. I called their parents."

Mark nodded and came inside. The house smelled like chicken cooking, and the radio was on in the living room.

"I expect retaliation," she said, and made a fierce face.

He followed her into the kitchen and took a beer from her. "Strange things have been happening to me," he said.

Anita said nothing for a moment. "Okay."

"I'm carrying around this thing inside me." He realized as he said it that he sounded a little loopy. "I got these pills from McCauley, and now I've got this space in my body. I mean, it *feels* like it. I don't actually have it. It's this huge space." He pulled up his shirt and showed her his belly.

Anita said, "A joke."

"No," he said. "Not at all. And I feel totally calm." He put down the beer and held out his hands. "See? No shaking."

Anita went to the oven, peered inside, then straightened up. Her frizzy hair was clamped back on her head today. "I'm waiting for the punch line."

"Artinium and floxisporum. That's what I'm taking."

"Okay."

"But it's huge." It was vast, vaster than it had ever been. Vast and dark, like a cave. "In here. It goes on forever."

"I'm expecting someone," she said. "I have a date."

"Oh," he said. "I'm sorry about the way I've been lately. I haven't been very kind."

"Fuck off, Mark," she said. "Go home."

"Okay." He held his hands up. "Have a good time." He edged himself out of the kitchen and back through the house. He expected to feel some sadness, but on the front walk he felt only a drop of something inside——a bright spot, a bit of fire, falling from his sternum to his navel—and then it was gone.

Friday morning he woke massive as ever. He rolled pregnantly out of bed and, with a small spurt of worry, remembered he was to go to the hospital today. Like anyone, he had a healthy fear of death, and his hands wavered a little as he dressed and examined his pouchy face in the mirror. He wondered, as he had wondered all week, whether he could fit behind the wheel of his Honda; but of course he could. He encountered no traffic and parked without difficulty, and in the fluorescent waiting room he was greeted with ominous cheer. Too quickly his name was called. The MRI machine, a long white tunnel, sat waiting against a wall. He eyed it warily, undressed to his waist, palming his precious middle. Another nurse, a tiny black woman this time, held out a tray. "No earrings, now, no tongue studs?"

"No," said Mark.

"Down you go," she said. "This is just a nice face mask to hold you still. Little shallow breaths through your nose. Eyes closed, no blinking."

He lay down plumply and after a moment began to slide backward. Feeling like a coffin on a conveyor belt, he had a moment of panic; then the white sleeve of the tunnel came down over his brow, and he closed his eyes. A gargantuan whirring began, and he sensed—heard—the magnets spinning in their toroid around his head. There came a faint, ghostly tugging, a vague inclination of the atoms of his brain to migrate to the edges of his skull. Disloyal things, he thought.

When it ended, he slid out again and opened his eyes.

"Perfecto," said the nurse, gazing at her screen.

"Anything wrong?"

"Well," said the nurse, "I'm not really supposed to say. But it looks good here. Nothing unusual."

He retrieved his shirt and peered over her shoulder. He saw a vertical slice of his brain: lobes of green and yellow, wiggles and spots—and there, at the red core of his soul, an eerily familiar Y-form, one flaming track rising toward the back of his head, another falling away toward the base of his neck. "Oh," he said. "Hello there." The seven of them, alive as they fell, he thought.

"A pretty thing, isn't it?" said the nurse. "Your very own brain."

That afternoon he saw the psychiatrist, Redmond Boxer, a very fat man with long, extravagant black hair. Boxer stood to meet Mark. "Mr. Horton," Boxer said. His cheeks were pink and bright, and he wore a dark green tie: a handsome man, all things considered. "Sit down," he said, and stood by the window, blocking a good deal of light.

"Thank you." Mark settled himself with care into the only chair.

"And what seems to be the trouble?"

He'd taken some pills, Mark said, and listed them. He described the space as best he could: the cavernous feel of it, the gravity it had given him. It was, maybe, because of the pills. But if it wasn't the pills—well, he didn't know what to make of it. "I could stop taking them, I suppose," he said. "But the doctor said they wouldn't do this. She thinks it's stress-related. I had my head scanned this morning. It doesn't look like there's anything out of the ordinary."

Boxer stood for a while at the window, silently regarding his desktop. Mark felt the minutes lengthen and gather.

Finally Boxer said, "So what is in this space?"

"Oh, nothing, exactly," Mark said. "It's not that sort of space."

"What do you mean?"

"It doesn't contain things."

"It's a special sort of space that doesn't contain things," Boxer said. "Unlike other spaces."

"I guess," Mark said. "It's big, though."

"Miles across, you say."

"Yes," Mark said. He felt a little absurd, pregnant with nothing. But it wasn't his fault, he thought; he hadn't done anything.

Boxer turned and touched the windowpane with his fingers, looked down into the parking lot. "It's not the worst thing to have, is it?"

"No."

"I have people who tell me they're suddenly afraid of their faces in the mirror," Boxer said. "Or trees. Suddenly they're afraid of trees, and frankly most of the time I don't know how to reply."

"I bet."

"You're in an interesting line of work, aren't you?"

"I like it," Mark said. He crossed his legs. "I've always liked it."

"Even when you had the accident. The crash."

"No. I didn't like it then."

"How awful that must have been." Boxer touched the knot of his tie. "Not your fault, of course. But nonetheless. The spectacle of it. Those poor, brave people."

"Lot of us quit the business."

"Not you."

"I'd only just started," he said. "My second year there."

"That makes a difference, I suppose."

"It did to me." Mark put his hands over his belly.

Boxer turned back to the window and hiked up his pants. "Well," he said.

Mark stood up. "I have a question." He took off his shirt and turned around. "Look at my spine for me."

Boxer approached, his shoes squishing under his weight. "What shall I look for?"

"A jog between my shoulder blades."

Boxer put his finger there. "No, it's perfectly straight."

"I thought it might be." He put his shirt back on and explained.

"Randolf-Doyle? There's no such thing. No such syndrome exists."

"I thought not." But he was calm, calm as the sky.

"No, I suspected you might have some sort of agoraphobia at first, but now I don't think so."

Mark sat down again. Somewhere in the building an elevator whirred, then stopped.

"For that, I usually have a suggestion. For agoraphobia."

"All right," Mark said.

"Which is, you get the largest room you can find," Boxer said, "and you sit there for an hour or so."

"Like an auditorium."

"Yes, or an arena of some sort. A hockey game, say." Boxer went over and sat down behind his desk. "You can afford a ticket somewhere, I imagine."

"Sure."

"The Thunderbirds are playing tonight, and I," said Boxer, "am a hockey fan."

"I'll come along."

Boxer steepled his fingers. "And, as a bonus," he said, "it's versus Medicine Hat."

The arena was cold and smelled like ice and hot dogs. Boxer chuffed up the stairs next to him, climbing to their seats.

"Home again," Boxer said, settling in.

They were early. Below them, the ice lay polished like a tabletop, and the teams, one in white, one in red, skated around and around. The referees skated, too, in long strides, around the perimeter of the rink. Bright lights burned overhead, and the crowd burbled around them. It was satisfying to be out again, Mark thought, out among people. Across the arena, at eye level, people sat looking back at him. He waved.

"See someone?" Boxer asked.

"No one in particular."

"How does this feel?" Boxer asked. "Any change?"

Mark paused to feel his belly, the space inside. "Not really. It's still there."

Boxer said, "Give it time."

"I wouldn't be sorry if it never went away, actually. It's a nice feeling."

"Perhaps we should leave?"

"No," said Mark. "It can't last forever, I guess."

After a while the game began, violent and raucous and very fast, the players moving in circles and the puck moving in lines. He'd never been to a hockey game before, and he liked the sound of it, the skidding and slapping, the wintry sound of the ice under the skates.

Boxer said, "I suppose you think me very unprofessional."

"It hadn't occurred to me."

"I *am* a professional, despite appearances," he said. "I have good spells, but this isn't one of them. Inviting you out like this."

Mark nodded. The game went on below, circling and circling. It was a beautiful thing to watch.

"If you want to go," Boxer said, "please feel free. I made all that up about the largest room. I just wanted someone to come with me tonight. I hate coming out alone."

"It's all right."

"You could sue me," said Boxer. "You'd be within your rights."

"I won't."

Boxer said, "Thank you."

"Don't mention it." The game went on.

Boxer breathed through his nose. "Crunchola," he said, now and then. At the end of the first period he said, "There's a sort of halftime show now. A man, that one there, is going to jump on his trampoline." A crew was sliding the thing out along the ice. "It's just a larky thing. Not any sophisticated show." The man wore a striped mime's outfit and minced comically across the rink, then hoisted himself up with great vigor and showmanship onto the leather edge and removed his sneakers. "I've seen him maybe a dozen times already," said Boxer. "He must get forty or fifty dollars a night, at the most. Really, it's sad. It always is, this bush-league entertainment. And yet he looks so happy. Mime on a trampoline. Imagine putting that on your résumé."

"Not much competition."

"No. Nor much demand."

With a flair the man raised his arms to the stands and stepped nimbly into the center of his apparatus, where he bounded once or twice before beginning to leap in earnest. Within moments he had gained a great height, the springs of the trampoline squeaking.

"He does get up there, I'll give him that," said Boxer.

"It must be dangerous."

The man rose, touched his toes, and sank back again. He pretended to ride a bicycle and looked out at the stands with grave calm. Getting off the bicycle, he brushed his teeth, checked his watch, and put up an imaginary umbrella. Then he began to swim.

"What a silly, silly man." Boxer laughed. "Imagine."

"Not a word."

"Who could hear him anyway? And what would he say? He's a fool."

"Up," said Mark.

"And a-down."

"And a-up."

"And a-down."

"Ha," said Mark, delighted. He didn't deserve this happiness, he thought. Alive as they fell. Counting down the altitude, according to some rumors, never confirmed. But the man in stripes was pushing himself higher and higher until at last he was at eye level, facing them both when he came to the briefest of rests at the top of his arc. He had stopped swimming and now just soared, his arms out. Mark, sitting pregnantly in the stands, palmed his belly—all the great spaces inside him—while outside, the man continued to rise and fall, rise and fall, flying the brave and populous air.

Michael Byers is the author of *The Coast of Good Intentions*. He is a former *Missouri Review* Editors' Prize winner for his first story publication.

MUSIC OF THE INNER LAKES/*Roger Sheffer*

FOR A LONG TIME I held my left hand in a fist. I held my right hand in a fist, too, as if to protect it from what had happened to the left that day in the Silver Lake store, when my cousin asked, "How thin do you want your turkey?" and I said, "I don't know." A careless gesture, bright blade spinning, the upper joints of my ring and pinkie fingers suddenly disconnected, suspended in air above the slicer, then dropping into a pool of blood.

After five years of self-pity, I opened both fists and gave serious thought to playing guitar again. I reversed the strings and began to retrain my left hand as the picking hand, stood in front of the mirror, made myself dizzy, then tried it with my eyes closed. No music. That was in July. After that, the guitar sat in its case, a shadowy object propped against the wall, pinheaded, bottom-heavy. Eventually I reversed the strings back to their normal sequence and made do with the chords that could be held down with two fingers, getting the thumb involved by reaching around to the sixth string.

"Such a coward," my cousin said as she bagged my groceries: packaged lunch meat, rye bread, beer, pretzels, mayonnaise, canned goods. Last night, scared of rowing across the lake in the rain, I had missed the weekly folk concert at the town museum.

"How were the fiddlers?" I asked.

"Absent. Sick. Food poisoning." Janine frowned at a can of chicken soup, obviously unsure of the price, dropped it into my pack without ringing it up, and waved her hand over the keys of the cash register as if to appease the god of commerce. "I wish you'd stop being a hermit and hook up your damn phone. When you don't show up on time for something, the first thing I assume is that your boat sank."

"It was supposed to rain."

"So? *I* went anyway. Your hair gets wet, no big deal. I'm about ready to shave mine all off, you know." She pulled the concert flyer from the side of the register, balled it up and tossed it into the trash, then clapped her hands, applauding either her good aim or the fact that the concert was over. "Other musicians came up and played, some bad, some good, if you trust my opinion. I took a blanket and sat on the lawn. No mosquitoes, and it didn't rain! At least not on our end of the lake. You would have loved it!" she raved. She slapped her left hand on the counter, kept a steady beat as she described the quartet who had come up on stage as the final act. "You *just* would have loved them."

She was talking about the Meekers, very backwoods locals, occasional store customers who bought gas and cigarettes, kerosene in winter. They paid cash only, no credit—and no food stamps, though they were surely eligible. They had a place twenty miles north of Silver Lake on a desolate road named for the family. Father, mother, brother, sister, they were folk performers of the most primitive kind. No instruments. Their purely vocal music was original, sorrowful, repetitive, shocking. They sang everything in octaves and fourths and fifths. "To this beat," Janine said, slapping the counter again with a forceful stare.

Half the show was how the family looked, she said, their heads stiff and eyes wide open, scared either by their own music or by the horrors the music described. "Look how mad you are. Ha! You really missed something!"

I *was* mad, but I was also disgusted with myself, with my failure to write any music for the past several years. I left the store still feeling mad at myself. When I got to my boat, there was an inch of water in it, a soggy towel, a popsicle wrapper. I set the backpack on the rear seat and grabbed the oars. I looked at my fingers. There might be a song in the horrors of slicing off fingertips, but I would change the story and have it take place on an isolated mountain, twenty miles from help: *My lover was trimming my fingernails. The jackknife slipped.*

Music was seeping back into my life; I felt the change and finally acted on it. The last concert evening of the summer, ninety percent chance of rain this time, I suddenly felt brave, rowed to the store, poked my head in and asked Janine if she'd go with me. She had overdue bills to pay, though, and waved me out the door with a fly swatter. So I drove six miles to the museum barn alone and sat on a bench and watched the fiddlers perform, a couple of old hippies, one with a long beard, the other ponytailed. They were okay, although when they put down their instruments to sing, their voices tended to sag—flat, waterlogged, unblended on the back vowels. Folk singing doesn't have to be bad singing, off pitch. It's supposed to sound good, and these guys didn't. It was a relief to get back to the lightness of their fiddling. I sat alone, cuddling my flask of rum. In my old singing days, I'd carried a flask inside my jacket and drunk from it between numbers to soothe my throat, loosen me up.

When the fiddlers had completed their set, the emcee invited audience members to come up and perform. "Hey, don't be shy, I know we got some fine singers out there!" he coaxed. I remained seated—I had not brought my guitar, couldn't play it anyway, and I had no songs, nothing but dried-out fragments, stuck in the mud of some isolated stream.

Then the Meekers made their entrance, unannounced, kind of shuffling and bumping into each other. It was warm that night, but they shivered and hugged themselves. They arranged their stiff bodies in a straight line, more than arm's length apart, as if spacing themselves to do calisthenics. Or they might have been pleading for new clothes. *Look at us. This is all we own.* The little girl had on pink shorts and a white T-shirt, yard-sale rejects. The other three were in jeans and flannel. The mother's hair was wet, flat, hacked. She had a bald spot. The father and son looked close enough in age to be brothers, and they carried themselves the same way—left shoulder low, head tipped to the right—and wore identical gray baseball caps, bills forward. They set up a rhythm by slapping their thighs, and the little girl sang a few measures before the men came in with a nasal drone: Jesus this and Jesus that, and *take me now, Lord Jesus.* I had hoped for better. They blended well, with the mother clapping through most of these numbers, singing alto on choruses, but the music was too gospel for me, too fiercely hopeful of salvation—which was what must have endeared them to Janine. Finally, the older of the two men cleared his throat and announced, "One more, everybody, then we'll scoot on home. It's called 'Don't Leave Me in the Snow,' and every word is true. Wrong time of year for a song like that, but maybe you'll feel it, if it's any good." He clapped a couple times, the girl started to sing, then he stopped her with a hand on the shoulder and said to the audience, "You're gonna want the background on this."

He described a dark little lake at the end of their property, where the road ended and a trail took over, a faint and ghostly footpath that wiggled through thirty miles of true wilderness before it hit the next road. One of his family—evidently there were at least a dozen members living out there—had hiked to the shore of this lake in early April that year, a few days before the ice went out. At the eastern end of the lake, a half mile away, maybe not even that far, two people came into view, stranded on the ice, waving, shouting for help. They broke through and went down slowly, still calling out as they sank, hands waving for a moment after the heads disappeared. The next day, the singer went on, he and his son had ventured out with their shepherd dog and tracked footprints ten miles northeast, up to an abandoned shack at the edge of the snowline. That was where they made a terrible discovery, he said. He stopped. "Heck, I'm ruining it for you," he said with a dark laugh. "We'd better sing the darn thing." So the men slapped their thighs and the little girl sang alone:

Father, Father, don't leave me in the snow.
I'm cold and hungry.
Father, Father, please don't go.
You seem so angry.

The other voices came in and acted out the parts—the father and the son who came down from the shack and got lost in the fog and scrubby underbrush, finally arriving at the lake and stepping onto the too-thin ice; the mother who stayed behind caring for her daughter until the little girl died and who then went crazy and wandered into the wilderness, into the endless deep snow. Mrs. Meeker hugged herself as she sang this part, almost weeping. The men kept up a good beat on the floor, heavy shoes drumming steady and solid, as the little girl became a ghost and the father and brother sank into the cold lake. The verses continued, no details omitted. These were the dead, telling their own story. It was a damn fine song.

While they sang and beat on the floor, I pressed my thumbnail into the tip of my left index and middle fingers, the ones that were still intact on that hand. They were soft, much too soft. I used to do this in the dentist's chair as a distraction from the prick of a Novocaine needle or the slip of a drill too close to a nerve. I leaned back and drank from my bottle. The audience clapped along, and the chorus, *Father, Father, don't leave me in the snow*, became so familiar that I belted out a line or two of it until the little girl gave me the evil eye. I had thrown them off for a measure. But they knew the song well, and I was only learning it, forming chords with missing fingers—E minor, C, D, B minor, phantom chords, invisible lines of concordance where the voices kept crossing and repeating.

The store lights were off. Janine had closed early and gone to bed. There were stars in the sky, no moon. I got into my boat, centered myself, laid the flashlight on the rear seat, pointing over the stern to illuminate the perfect wake. I found myself humming the Meekers' ballad as I rowed, and I kept beat with the oarstrokes, hardly noticing when the rain began to fall again, hardly feeling the chill. Far to the east, moving toward the point, two sets of headlights stitched a hem along the dark skirt of the lake.

The words of one of the final verses came back to me. They told how the Meekers had found the girl's cold, barefoot body in the shack, on a stained mattress. She gripped a hairless rag doll so tightly that she had to be buried that way. The old stove was slightly less cold than every other surface. Someone had burned pages from a Bible in it. Ice had formed in a lower corner, and caught in that ice was a dead mouse, lying on its back.

I had already hiked most of the trails in the county and marked them in brown on my 1945 map over the faint, broken lines representing older trails, many of which had faded away in the years since the map was drawn—ghost trails. Meeker Road lay beyond my usual range. It was my rule never to drive more than twice as far as I intended to hike: drive ten miles to the trailhead, then walk at least five miles in; drive twenty, then walk at least ten, but ten was pushing my physical limit for day hikes, and I never carried a sleeping bag or stove, never slept in the woods. Too much of a coward, I told Janine.

But my cousin had not been up where the Meekers lived in many years, and she wanted to go there. In the dead time between Labor Day and peak color, she turned off the gasoline pumps and closed the store for an afternoon. "You have to come," she told me. "This is much more of an adventure than going to a little concert at the barn."

We drove parallel to the winding river, past the old ski area and over the divide into balsam country, with only an occasional flare of maple red to remind us of the season. As we drove, we speculated about the Meekers. Janine said, "I'm probably related to them. We had a renegade cousin up here in the woods, a long time ago."

"So it's in the blood!" In my best voice I sang the chorus for her: *"Father, Father, don't—"*

"My blood. Not yours. And mine's very much thinned out, I'm sure."

I tapped the steering wheel with my mangled fingers, where she could see them. "You don't like my singing."

"It's just that one person can't do four-part harmony."

Meeker Road was paved for the first hundred yards, after which the rough asphalt turned to dirt. Yellow signs marked the curves or warned of a narrow bridge, a hairpin turn, children at play. We passed a trailer that was nearly lost among scaly wooden additions, then a DEAF CHILD AREA sign, faded almost to white, bullet-riddled and perhaps no longer necessary. There might be a song in how that had happened: *Father, Father, please don't shoot, I couldn't hear you.*

"Who's the deaf child?" I asked.

"Buddy Meeker. He's almost thirty now, finally graduated high school. At least they gave him a diploma."

"Not one of the singing Meekers."

Janine shook her head.

The road narrowed to one lane under a canopy of beech and ancient white pine, with loose gravel and grass down the median, not much more than a jeep trail. There was a tarpaper cabin on the right, an old bus on the left and a sagging gray house straight ahead. The road dead-ended there, with no space to turn the car around. There had to be dogs out here, I thought, mad dogs, half coyote, chained up—or maybe not chained up. No sign that this was the Meeker place. No mailbox with musical notes painted on it. Nothing like that.

"They're not home," Janine said.

"Maybe they're touring," I joked. "Gone to Nashville."

"Right. If they block our car, we'll be forced to talk to them." She rolled up her window. "They might let their dogs out, or something worse."

"Let's hike. We'll meet them in the woods."

"So you're not such a coward," she said, looking at me with sudden interest.

Well, I had my fears. But the air smelled so nice and sweet, and my mind was clearing. I was ready for just about anything.

We locked the car and began hiking a dry path into the state wilderness. Janine knew the territory—the ghost towns, the tanneries and sawmills that had thrived a hundred years ago, the small upland lakes formerly connected by road to the outer world. A single overgrown trail now threaded that mysterious fabric. Janine pointed to the remnants of stone walls, property lines. This was old farmland, never productive of anything except misery—too rocky, too steep, too cold. An ancestor from the last century, another poor cousin had who lived in this valley, had gone out to chop wood one morning, Janine reminded me. "And froze solid, standing up, axe in midswing."

"That's folklore," I laughed.

"It's a good story," Janine said. "Write a song about it. If you don't want it, I'll give it to the Meekers next time they come to the store."

I didn't see any lake where the Meekers' song claimed it would be, only a swamp. The trail followed a stream, outlet from a chain of lakes that lay ten miles east of us. Janine called them the "inner lakes," her voice sucking in after the *s* and her mouth clamping shut tight, as if she thought that by saying it that way she could actually contain the water of the lakes. The property had been owned by her father's family until the twenties, sold to International Paper, then to the state; all structures had been removed at that time. More were built later, though, illegally—hunting shacks, tent platforms, lean-tos cobbled out of wrecked snowmobiles and broken skis—by loners who shopped for food once or twice a year. Janine did business with such men, said she assumed they had families from what they bought: the toys, women's magazines, crossword puzzle books, children's aspirin, a case or two of infant formula. They paid cash, these men from the inner lakes. They never spoke, hardly breathed through their thick beards.

"Lost River," she said, her voice sucking in again.

"Good name for another song."

"Oh, don't bother. The Meekers already wrote it. Everything they wrote came out of this godforsaken place." In fact, she told me, they had sung "Lost River" the evening I stayed home, afraid of the rain. "Lost River," Janine repeated. She picked up a dead branch and flung it toward the stream, waited for the splash. "*Lost River, Lost River,*" she chanted, "*Hid away, where grandpa lay, darkest day, darkest day . . .*"

Damn those Meekers. I wanted a virgin trail to take me into this part of my life, or, if not virgin, at least not so heavily traveled in recent years. I didn't want to keep hearing that some other party had arrived ahead of me, grabbed all the good songs and sung them in public. Janine lagged behind as the path got steeper. In her pale, flat voice, she sang for a while, alone, and then with the wind accompanying her, blowing across the hard edges of a well-tuned forest.

Whenever I hiked, I carried a stick, dead wood, a device to measure the measureless, that broke off in segments if it struck something hard. There was a music in that, a music in walking, in the shifting and dimming light that came down through the trees, now mostly yellow birch and hemlock. There was music in crossing the contours of this upland, as I had seen them drawn on a map, tight and parallel like a musical staff, five lines for every hundred feet of elevation. It was as if the whole landscape were fretted. We climbed higher, hearing the sound of water falling across the resistant rock, noting the tree roots that held back the soil in even steps and feeling—at least I did—as if we were going back in time, across years and decades, time held back by the regrowth of the forest and the narrowing of the trail.

It's too late, I said to myself. I meant late in the day, but it was late in the year, too, late in the decade. My dead stick was entirely gone, all the pieces scattered, and if I wasn't careful, I'd soon be breaking off finger-tips. We'd have to turn around soon, even though by now we had begun to follow footprints, frozen hard in this dry mud, toes pointed downhill, toward us.

And I would have turned around if I hadn't seen a set of prints in fresh mud, toes pointed the other direction, into the wilderness. They were sneaker prints, child-size, not much bigger than my hand, and so clear that they looked as if they had been deliberately placed there as false evidence. The muddy stretch ended. There were dry leaves, and the sneaker prints disappeared as the trail shot up over a piney ridge and then back down toward the creek, which was roaring now with the water that had spilled down from the inner lakes. We were two miles in, maybe more. I thought of how she had said it, the s at the end of lakes, drawn out like static that covered a truth she would not articulate—a truth always withheld from me. I stopped for a minute, called out, "Janine!" and then moved ahead slowly, waiting for her reply. The creek was too loud. I grabbed another walking stick.

When the roar of the creek subsided, a drumming took over, or an axe slowly chopping. I called out for Janine again. The drumming seemed too musical to be an axe. It might have been some animal language, a huge bird warning me off, or a couple of big-horned sheep knocking their heads together.

A sharp turn in the trail revealed a skinny boy in ragged gray shirt and black jeans, whacking a big stick against a hollow tree trunk.

I coughed, then called out, but he didn't hear me. I shouted, "Whatcha doing?" and he still didn't turn to answer. I tapped his shoulder with my walking stick, and he swung, wielding his stick like a sword.

I remembered the Meekers' deaf son. "Are you Buddy?" I asked.

He held the stick in front of his chest, mouth open, and grunted in a low voice. He was the strangest-looking kid I'd ever seen, with his continuous eyebrow, dirty blond cave-man hair, ears sticking out much too high on his head, like a cat's. He might have been twelve, fourteen, eighteen . . . even twenty-eight. He might have been a Meeker or some-thing more primitive, of which the Meekers were a cleaned-up version sent out into the world to perform. Whatever he was, I thought, he was the kind of thing they had been singing about. Except for a slight tremor in my maimed fingers, I did not move, afraid he would hit me with his stick.

He said nothing. He was painfully skinny, concave. There were welts on his face and neck.

"I'm sorry," I finally said, and the boy seemed to relax, dropped his stick, scratched his funny ears. I set down my stick and held out my empty hands, a gesture of peace. He smiled and reached into the hollow tree, from which he pulled a handful of swarming beetles of some kind, held them out for my inspection and after a couple seconds shoved them in his mouth. The bugs seemed to vibrate inside his neck for a second before he swallowed them, buzzing for that brief moment, more articulate than any sound he could make. That's what I thought about, not the grossness of it. He pounded his chest, reached into the tree trunk again and pulled out another handful, offering them to me. I stepped back and shook my head. He ate the bugs, then grabbed his stick and took off, northeast, deeper into the wilderness, his feet hardly touching the ground.

That was it. No doubt, I thought, there were more freaks like him higher up, hidden: conjoined twins, people with dog heads, chicken heads, a world of wonder that had never been set to music. Yes, I would have followed the boy to it if not for Janine.

"Are you lost—are you lost—are you lost—are you lost?" Janine's anxious voice echoed through the valley as I stood by the hollow tree, drumming a beat with my walking stick. Bang, bang, pause. Bang, bang, pause. I was deep in this place now, deep and rooted in the place where the songs began, the place where I would begin to write again. I kept beating, as if to coax a melody out of the tree trunk. The dead wood had a definite tone that rang back through my arms and into my whole body. Low E-flat. Very low. An owl hooted somewhere nearby, mad at me, or oblivious to my presence. B-flat. Another bird sounded as if it were crying—two notes, C and F, the second note dropping. "Are you lost—are you lost—are you lost?" Already I was making a song of those words, setting them to the rhythms and notes that I had picked up. The sad part about the song was that, in many ways I was still standing on the surface of this world. I had not broken through.

I lay down in pine needles and rolled to one side. Some of the needles poked into my left ear and strummed three chords along the very top of my hearing. The upper branches of a dead beech, shaped like a disfigured hand, raked across the deep blue sky, and I heard that, too.

Roger Sheffer is a finalist in this year's Editors' Prize Contest. His third collection of fiction will be published this fall.

ON THE NATURE OF STARLINGS/
Morri Creech

for my grandfather

More than the fronds of silk trees feathering down
on the front lawn, or the slant light burnishing
the hoods of junked cars in the pasture,
more than the banked fires at the field's edge
and the smoldering leaves, for you autumn
stretched its wing over the tin roofs and corn rows
when the first starlings slipped down to comb
the still-flourishing landscape, stripping
the ripe kernels or scrawled like scripture
across the branches of evergreens. Theirs
was the sure precision of appetite—though often
from roadsides and windows you admired
their industry, how they gleaned
from slag heaps and shards of bottle glass
the least grain or morsel of fallen seed.
Black threads stitching the cloth of heaven,
to hear them calling from the barn roof
or weathervane was to know the raw music
of grief, or so you believed, as though each loss
lay upon your heart like a glossy feather;
so that what I wanted to tell you this afternoon
as I stood in the garden and watched them
hunt for strewn seeds and settle without hesitation
on the sleeve of the scarecrow
was that, surely, this is how absence
accumulates, starling by starling, wing by wing
reconstituted as elegy—and though I could not
quite remember or hear your one voice
above the din of that raucous choir, I wanted
to listen for a moment, and to praise them
if only for their stubborn persistence,
for how they flock at the margins of memory
and will not scare, no matter how the dark drops down
feather by feather, dismantling the light.

THE HEAVEN OF MEMORY / *Morri Creech*

for John Wood

For example, say the world is nothing more
than this rinse of light in autumn under oak limbs,
the shade-swept brilliance of things
both as they are and as they are remembered,
with those few birds perched on the clothesline
neither mimicking the regal flight of shirts and overalls
nor ferrying the spirit homeward
to the shrill articulations of grief and loss,
but hunkered over the laundry and fallen leaves,
repeating their coarse, discordant syllables.
For the sake of argument, say the starling's wing
is all we shall ever know of the colors
of heaven; say the soul is a breath made visible
on the cold air, or that the promised end,
like some ripe Miltonic fruit shimmering
on a far branch, tastes of ash before it disappears.
The truth is, no matter how brilliant the logic
of seasons, no matter how sternly we renounce
the harsh God of insomnia and thunder,
something tempts us toward the infinite,
toward a gilded future embellished from memory:
streets paved brick by brick from the ore
of nostalgia, a photographic silver
where everything we've loved is restored
to its flawed perfection: tart apples
from the tree beside the old house, wisteria
of childhood scenting the hallowed air.
And what if heaven is nothing but desire?
Even so, from that common seed we cultivate
our thoroughly inhabitable kingdoms;
and the mind, a place of its own, in itself
shapes from the earth its makeshift paradise.

VERNACULAR / *Morri Creech*

Was it always there
            with us failing
to hear it?

—R. S. Thomas

And when he listened
it was like wind that rinses the first bird-notes from the
    larch trees,
winnows the pollen from leaf-down,
sows witch grass and thistle,
that harrows the surface of the waters,
that in summer is the slow fever of mosquitoes and
    rivershine
and in winter snags the ribs of scattered leaves,
that plays the low notes of the locust's wing
and, formless itself, imposes
upon the forms of limestone and hollowed reeds,
that unravels its story
to the acres of fence line and pasture,
to the sun-cluttered joists and rafters of bankrupted
    churches,
that in childhood is a sweetness
at the tops of the sycamores
and in adulthood a remembrance of sweetness
among dried sheaves and the one cardinal's feather
splayed in the field, that swells to a consummate music
and contracts to a held breath,
that is balm of the honeysuckle,
balm of clover and mint,
that stirs bees from their hives
and wasps from their paper cathedrals,
that forges its burnished imprint on the river,
that sculpts an absence,
sculpts the one syllable held in the dumb mouths of
    statues,
that raises only its own name,
praises its own dust,
and hastens toward the silence of its own beginnings.

LANDSCAPE OF HEAVEN / *Morri Creech*

Once mustard is sown, it is scarcely possible to be free
of it; for the seed germinates at once when it falls.
                                                    —Pliny the Elder

And he said, Whereunto shall we liken the kingdom of God?
                                                    —Mark 4:30

Like coarse flame consuming the garden
they sway their braided tongues—
fierce, innumerable. Weeds, you say,

meaning those tattered stalks
that ravage the foxglove and columbine.
Yet imagine a heaven of weeds:

mustard whelming the extravagant lilies
and marigolds, spending field after field in its strict
profusion, like the necessary violence of God.

Perhaps it's true that love of the world
is another way to enter paradise,
that force and beauty are equal under heaven.

But here, in the landscape of weeds, amid the wrestle
of stem and root, dying is the wages
of mercy. And in the kingdom they compose,

all things—bramble and burdock,
the flax's sun-scorched petals—
are defined by the light that touches them.

HONEY AND JOHN THE BAPTIST /
Morri Creech

When the torn veil of the heavens
closed and mended,
when the clamor and delirium of angels
at once fell silent
and the crowds had gone,
what work was I left to do,
having set it all in motion,
having so long tasted
the sting of the sacred word
on my bestial tongue?

No longer chosen,
I staggered into the wilderness
and knelt at the split trunk
of the honey tree,
broke open the comb,
and blessed
with the pure praise of appetite
the fruits of earth I found there,
while the gospel went on
spinning its slow mysteries.

What did it matter?
Elsewhere in the desert
Christ, hungry and alone,
held in his palm
the small body of a scorpion,
weighing its form
against the emptiness.
And weren't the long beams of the cross
already hewn from the tree,
Salome's young thighs
ripening toward the dance

as I ate of the honey,
as I tasted the scald of bees
drowned in the chambered sweetness
of their own making?

DOGWOOD / *Morri Creech*

So this is what remains
of Christ in winter,
after the wounded petals
have dried and scattered
and the blown red leaves blaze
earthward. My father
told me its trunk once bore
the savior's body,
and for years I believed
the shadow of the one
outside my window
passed over me in judgment.

All season it brooded
over my mother's flowerbed,
her cabbage roses and hydrangeas,
long after she left my father.
And though he pulled
the slick maze of their roots
from the ground
next spring, he let the tree
abide there in the shade
of its own flourishing,
knelt and labored in silence
as the branches swelled
with patience and light.

Rooted half in soil, half in rumor,
warped tree of the garden,
for years the cleft in its trunk
has divided the twin boughs
of my belief and doubt.
Every night that winter
my prayers ascended its crown
and found no answer,
just as I imagine my father
prayed for strength or love.

Every night its bare limbs
scraped against the house
and blackbirds settled
in the heaven of its branches.

PROVISION / *Morri Creech*

Nothing we tried could coax sweetness
from my grandfather's apple tree.
Year after year we tended the branches,
propped the broken boughs with scraps of lumber.
Year after year those hunched limbs
dragged the ground and bore a withered fruit
nothing could eat, not even the neighbor's horses.
So who cared when, one winter, lightning
tore a smoldering seam down its trunk?
My grandfather left the tree alone all season,
figuring the rain-soaked husk not fit for burning.

That April, axes in hand, we crossed the field
to clear the warped remains. My grandfather
leaned down and stuck his hand inside
the storm-struck hollow, as though
to touch the blighted heartwood.
He jerked his hand back, cursing, wringing fire
from his palm—and as we ran toward the house
the whole tree seemed to come alive at once,
swarming and quickening with bees
that had settled there to make honey in the wound.

Morri Creech has poems published or forthcoming in *Poetry, Southern Review, Sewanee Review* and elsewhere.

GRASP SPECIAL COMB/*Stephanie Rosenfeld*

PEDICULOSIS: IDENTIFICATION AND TREATMENT
by Katherine Randall-Hillman

Pediculus humanis capitus, the common

—Return library books—UC Science lib: Pediculosis, pediculicides, pyrethrin, permethrin
—Call Mom

PEDICULOSIS AND YOUR CHILD
by Katherine L. Randall

—Buy bagels
—Check to V. Sch. of Ballet

PEDICULUS HUMANIS CAPITUS: ONE WILY MOTHERF— (Ha.)

—Ariadne: New leotard
                Ponytail holders
—Call Mom

YOUR CHILD AND HEAD LICE
by Kathy Hillman

Head lice is a common childhood _____ that can be present in any
segment of the population at any given time.

—disease, illness, malady, condition. Affliction.
—Afflict: to humble, overthrow, try, torment, torture, rack.
—Personal nuisance problem (Hamp. Cty, DPH)

—Rack (!)—Racked with lice

If your child comes home from school with head lice, don't be
alarmed

—Pharmacy: Nix (big size)
                      Egg dissolver stuff
                      Metal comb (check w/Gary—did he take mine?)
                      More of those plastic clampy things
—Cash

If your child comes home from school with head lice, try not to be alarmed

—Do laundry (check w/Ed re: why no hot H_2O?)
—Borrow vacuum (check w/Gary—why does he get vacuum; split cost of new one?)
—Ariadne: Cancel play date w/Chiara
                  " " w/Katrin
                  Practice
                  Wash and comb
—Comb Leon?
—Call Leon: Does he have magnifying glass at work?

If your child comes home with head lice, try not to panic

—Call Mom
—Grocery store: More laundry det.
                          Garbage bags (big)
                          Dinner??
                          Treat for Ariadne
—Video/book-on-tape for A. (unabridged)

If your child comes home with head lice

THE TRUTH ABOUT HEAD LICE
by Kathy Randall

Head lice is a scourge from hell that will temporarily ruin your life and possibly damage it permanently.
Kind of strong. Stick to facts.

Head lice, *Pediculus humanis capitus*, are tiny black, gray or brown
    —tiny insects, very difficult to see, which
      —insects so small it's difficult to see them at all, let alone tell
      what color they are

—tiny, moving, transparent, black-hearted specks and their eggs, malevolent grains of next-to-nothingness that attach themselves to the hair shaft at the scalp's surface and have the capacity to rob you of every crumb of hope, peace of mind, optimism or spiritual ease you might at one time have possessed, not to mention sanity, sleep and every free moment from the present to some far-off point in the increasingly unimaginable nit-free future.

There are a number of over-the-counter remedies available, all of which are extraordinarily expensive and none of which work. Their packages are printed with blatant lies, which a perky member of your HMO's advice staff ("This is Donna in A.S.") will read over the phone until you realize the words sound familiar. You ask if anyone there's ever actually had lice. You ask if anyone there's ever seen your child's head of hair when Miss A.S. says people do survive this, all you have to do is comb every strand of your child's hair two times each day, wash all the bedding in hot water every day, vacuum the entire house and the car every day. "Steam cleaning works best," she reads, "or simply close off the entire area: playroom, TV room—anywhere the kids spend a lot of time—for fourteen days."

She tells you, as if this is the way stupid people get lice in the first place, not to let children share brushes, clothing or headgear, and says, "There *is* a prescription available, but we don't like to use it except as a last resort," as if she wants you to beg her for a substance that will give your child permanent nerve damage. You say, "Headgear, Miss Verbatim?" you tell her you're guessing that she doesn't have any children, ask her how many rooms in her mansion. You ask what A.S. stands for again, Attitude Spewing? then thank her for the "advice" and hang up.

This is day two of lice; this is before you understand that lice can be used to measure many things: the shortness of a day; the ferocity of your instinct to kill things that attack your child; the natural amounts of pessimism and optimism you possess; the number of days remaining in your life.

—What happened to facts?
—Check w/ Gary re: health coverage after divorce
—Call Mom

FACTS
—Lice range from 2mm–4mm in size. Life cycle from nit to adult is 16 to 21 days. Adult lice live about 30 days. They

will die of starvation if kept off their host's body for more than 10 days. Cannot survive temperatures above 128.3 °F for more than 5 minutes.

—Lice need the blood of human beings to survive and will die naturally within 24 hours if they cannot find human blood.

—Which is it: 10 days or 24 hrs.?

—Female head louse glues eggs to the base of hairs. Will deposit 50–150 eggs in her lifetime. Eggs hatch in 5–10 days. Human hair grows about ½ inch per month. Therefore, any nits found on a hair ¼" from scalp would be approximately 16 days old and probably will not hatch.

—Cancel hair appt.

FACTS

—Anyone can get lice regardless of his/her degree of personal hygiene

—Caucasian children most likely to have lice

—Lice can affect you mentally (explain)

Lice might make you remember strange, unrelated things. Cooties, cootie spray, being a kid; sitting in the woods in Memory Grove with Maddy Jacobs and Jimmy Colon talking about the ghost people claim to be able to see there at night, walking across the road. Either she was a jilted bride or got hit by a car or both. Maddy saying, Let's play Flip Your Top, giving instructions: you pull your shirt up, just for a second, so Jimmy can see underneath. You remember being confused about a few things, like the way you felt when she said, "You *have* to." You believed the words were true, and it gave you kind of a sick ache, almost as if your life were over. It's the same thing you'll feel when you get lice, when it's six-thirty and dinner's not even started and you realize there's still all the bedding to wash—all the sheets and pillowcases and the towels, at the laundromat, no less, since Gary got to keep the appliances—before anyone can go to bed tonight. You *have* to. Why didn't Jimmy have to do anything? Why did he get to sit there, his face impassive, and watch you expose your lumpy, embarrassing chest?

—Too personal(?) Get back on the track.

Even though the memories it brings up aren't that great, lice might make you wish you were a kid again. The year of the great fruit-and-nut war—crabapple, plum, horse-chestnut fights on the way home from school. Any ripe, rotting, eye-sized projectile you could get your hands on. Always boys against girls. You might suddenly, intensely miss the manic abandon of that time, that state of grace, the intense, single-minded will to do damage to the enemy, without thought of consequence.

—Cancel Jessica for Saturday night / Can she baby-sit some-
time late Nov.?
—Cancel Ariadne dentist
—Call Mom

Or trying on bathing suits at the mall with your best friend, Denise, complaining about your moms—you might suddenly remember that.

Combing Ariadne's hair in the graying afternoon light, remembering trying on red bathing suits with Denise, the year of the Farrah Fawcett poster, in adjacent dressing rooms at Nobby in the Fashion Place Mall, sending the words up over the walls of the stalls: "Judy turned my white cords pink in the wash and she won't even give me money to buy another pair," "I swear to God Shirley's going through the change," you might get an unexpected pang, something wandering off in a wrong direction; you might suddenly wish for someone—even the person whose goal in life, you knew, was to make you think you were insane—to take care of you, your mother.

—What is the prob.?!! Get back to facts.

—Difference betw. head lice & body lice.
—Crabs.

Or it might make you remember college: it might make you think about your best friend, Randi. Denise is long gone by this time, engaged to a Mormon, friends with her mother. Randi took notes in Modern American Literature once on a box of Nilla Wafers she ate on the way to class.

"We're going to be late," you complained as you stood in line at the Sunshine Farms at eight in the morning, waiting for her to buy the cookies.

"So go," she said. But there was something about Randi—you couldn't leave her, bleary-eyed in her huge sweatshirt and boxer shorts, at the checkout.

"What's white and crawls up your leg?" Randi said. Something on one of the shelves had caught her eye. "Uncle Ben's Perverted Rice," she answered herself.

That's the kind of thing you might remember, sitting in front of *Pippi in the South Seas*, combing strand by strand: you might start thinking about how romance, marriage, whatever it is you are attempting to do with your boyfriend, that you attempted to do with boys back then, obscures most other kinds of love. And how Randi cracking her joke, not even looking at you but smiling into the corner, your presence required but not acknowledged, was a kind of love, though you didn't know it at the time: offered sideways, received quietly, an underlying condition and not a daily negotiation, and what does that have to do with lice? What does that have to do with you, as you sit in the darkening living room, combing Ariadne's hair? She is trying to be good, but tears leak out of the corners of her eyes. The health center literature suggests, "Keep squirmy kids in place with a Popsicle"; what kid wouldn't see this as a bogus non sequitur? You start to laugh.

"Why are you laughing, Mom?" Ariadne says, crying, then laughing a little, too.

"I had this friend once in college." You have never told Ariadne about Randi.

"What was she like?"

You try to remember what, about Randi, would be appropriate to tell a child. Once, drunk and high on coke, the two of you shot a tube of toothpaste in a fraternity bathroom with a bow and arrow. At a party at a different fraternity, Randi walked past a boy who had dumped her and said, in a conversational tone just loud enough for everyone to hear, "Dave Cooney? Premature ejaculator."

"Does Randi have kids?" asks Ariadne.

"A little girl, Sarah, I think."

Ariadne thinks about this for a minute, then says, "Maybe Sarah has lice, too."

—Product info. instead?
    Nix—permethrin; low toxicity, kills lice and eggs in one 10-minute treatment
    Rid—pyrethrin-based, not as effective at killing nits
    Kwell—lindane, prescription only, also not as good at killing nits. (Yet is more toxic. What is deal?)
    Malathion lotion—must stay on head for 8–12 hours.
—Problems re: putting a product called Malathion lotion on your child's head for 8–12 hours.

FACTS

—Nix is 95 percent effective (according to Nix). Its lice-killing effects continue to work for up to 14 days. May be used again after 7–10 days. (Not necessary, but recommended.)

—Lice can be eliminated from unwashable items by sealing in a plastic bag minimum of 14 days. However, 35 days is better to eliminate risk from any dormant egg.

—Dormant egg?

If your child comes home from school with head lice, try not to panic. There are over-the-counter products, called pediculicides, that claim

They all claim to kill lice and their eggs, but it's a crock! There is always one left alive. Every mother you talk to will look at you with round eyes, twitching head, and say, "They lie. The packages lie. I put a whole bottle of (X) on (Olivia/Elspeth/Ariel's head), and the next day a LIVE BUG walked across her scalp."

There are several over-the-counter products, that, combined with careful (thorough, vigilant, scrupulous, maniacal)

A special fine-toothed comb must be used to remove nits. Divide hair into 1-inch squares. Grasp special comb at an angle, with smooth side slanted backward

You can throw around the expressions "nit-picking" and "go through with a fine-tooth comb," but until your child actually comes home with lice, you can't really appreciate the meaning of the words; you will feel foolish, sheepish, for having used them lightly; you will feel annoyed, enraged, murderous toward people who commit this offense.

"*Have you really*?" you might say to your boss when he says he's been going over the payroll with a fine-tooth comb and uncovered a little problem in your department.

"*A fine-tooth comb,*" you say. Lice makes you talk in italics; it makes you impatient with the people you loathe. It wipes out the pleasantries, zooms you right to the heart of things. "*Interesting you should put it that way.*"

"These are *baked goods* we're talking about, right?" you might say when he says he wasn't going to mention it, but now that you've taken everything to such a negative level, yesterday's cookies were too big. "It's not like I put the baboon heart in the wrong patient, though, is it?"

you might say. You might actually yell that. "It's not like anyone *died, right?* It's not like anyone *got lice.*"

When your boss says he's putting you on notice, you jump up from the table. *"You're* putting *me* on notice. That's rich!" Lice makes you sound like Fred Flintstone.

You put all the men in your life on notice.

"Oh, when I'm *nit-picking* you'll know it," you blurt to your up-till-now-perfectly-good boyfriend when he chooses the unfortunate phrase to tell you you remind him of his mother.

"What do *you* know about *nit-picking?*" you imagine yourself challenging the next boyfriend, the one in the unimaginable future. Even men from the past—all the old boyfriends who left for one reason or another—suddenly fall into one of two new categories: those who could have weathered an infestation with you, and the rest.

—(Lice as evolutionary tool in boyfriend selection)

Lice might cause you to dissociate more than usual; you might find yourself thinking about the desert, where you once lived; you can picture the lice dying of dehydration, falling backward off your head like staggering movie bad guys. You can feel your scalp baking in the cleansing heat; hear the trickle of water, like a new beginning, in a dry wash.

You might picture these things while your boyfriend is screaming, "*I* didn't bring lice into this house!" It is the day after the first treatment and combing. He has reached his limit already.

You have slipped and said that the one set of clean sheets is "at home." In your dryer, in your ex-husband's house. Technically still your house too. "In the dryer," you say. "Gary's dryer. *My* dryer. For God's sake. Whatever." It gets confusing. Technically, also, Gary is not yet your ex. You will get around to getting divorced one day soon. After the refinancing goes through and the lice are gone.

"I don't really like the doing-laundry-at-Gary's thing," he's said again. He's mentioned it a few times in the past year. It makes him uncomfortable to think there's some kind of unspoken connection lingering between you and Gary, and he would prefer it if you lugged your laundry, and Ariadne's, to the laundromat.

You warned this man, when he was pursuing you, "It's not going to be the way you think it's going to be."

"Let's go to Baja," he said. Morocco, Indonesia, the Golden Triangle. Hot, sultry nights; the two of you in a little shack on the beach or in the jungle, lying in a bed canopied by mosquito netting, reading books by candlelight, listening to short-wave radio.

"I've never been in a long-term monogamous relationship before," he said. "I'd really like to try it with you." He was surprised by your response, angry.

"Is that supposed to sound like a qualification to me?" you asked.

You don't say to him now that if he doesn't like the idea of the doing-the-laundry-at-Gary's thing, then he really wouldn't like the idea of the other thing, which you haven't told him: how a certain cold reality set in when you found the nits in your own hair, how when you called him at work to find out what time he'd be home to help you with them and he said, "I don't know; I was planning to stay a little late and look up some airfares on the Internet," you hung up and drove directly to the pharmacy and then to Gary's, where you shed your clothes in his bathroom and summoned him in to do the washing.

"Massage into hair, saturating every strand," you said to Gary, not even bothering to try to strike the note of gentleness his shrinking soul always required and never got from you. "Really, Gary. Don't dick around. Just get them out."

You hated the way Gary's hands felt in your hair, tentative and ineffectual, like always, which was reassuring. You both know you've made the right decision, though sometimes other people try to tell you you haven't. You must still have feelings for each other, they say. You seem to like each other.

Lice has an odd power, you are starting to discover, to show you things about your life.

For example, right there in the tub, you had a realization, suddenly, after all these years of separating from Gary: that you will be able to go forward to life without Gary, but it will never be possible to go back. You can't get rid of the facts: that Gary watched you give birth to Ariadne—propel a child out of your body, vomit, piss on the floor, bellow like an elephant, walk around afterward naked and moaning, your breasts rock hard and blue with engorgement, bigger than his head.

You think about the lingering, romantic, newly-in-love feelings that up until now still graced the atmosphere of your home with the boyfriend; you think about their sudden loss of substantiality, their lack of fortitude. You picture them as dropouts of a boot camp run by lice.

Another of the powers of lice is that it is placing unfamiliar words in your brain. "I can *do* this," you hear yourself thinking. You've come a long way from the days of driving around, crying, with baby Ariadne strapped in the back seat. It is not a comforting thought, just new information for your life: whatever impossible, unimaginable task you are called upon to do, you can do.

—Call Tinka Potter re: PTO "Oktoberfest" Committee—get
off my back

You might start to notice something: if there is a problem in your life, lice will reveal it as surely as—

Say your mother's in town, too. Say she's come to stay for two months, or as your boyfriend says, "TWO MONTHS!" which sounded, somehow, in February, over the telephone, not like the terrible idea it actually is.

Add to this the fact that you are a baker by "trade," a word your mother likes to employ to distinguish your job from other kinds of jobs, say like hers: Professional Poet; then factor in a lice infestation. Ariadne has just been sent home from school with a second round of lice—three weeks, three poisonous shampooings, thirty-six loads of laundry and forty-two combings into the ordeal—even though you've instructed her not to take off her cap, not to undo her braided bun, not to hug, touch or brush up against another human being until this is all over. It will seem then, in some strange way, exactly perfect—the final brilliant brushstroke on some perverse dream masterpiece—that when you arrive home from work ("You must be *tired*," your mother says, meaning, after your day of low-paid toil) she has made, there in your kitchen, a blueberry pie. Caved in, pallid, just like the pies of your childhood. Which (the childhood) she has come to hold against you all: you, your brother, your dead father. "Back when I was a cookie-pusher in Salt Lake" is the way she refers to that time.

"Guess what makes my crust so flaky?" she warbles now. You can see that your dish drainer's been emptied, your sink cleaned, your newspapers neatly stacked.

"*Lard, Mother?*" you whisper savagely, not in the mood to hear the familiar rendering (ha) of the amazing properties of lard, first part in a set piece, the second part of which features your mother as innocent shiksa newlywed feeding lard crust to her unsuspecting Jewish mother-in-law, which makes you think of your dead father, whose hair—thick, black, curly, oily—was a fascination to you.

"Yuck, Kathy," he'd say when you picked up his special silver-plated, soft-bristled hairbrush. You loved to smooth its bristles across your own head. "Don't touch that." Which made no sense at all: it was the same hair that tickled your face when you hugged him, that you put your hands in when you rode on his shoulders. It was your mother, you knew, who had done it—you remember the face she made when he scratched his head, as if she were watching to see whether anything would fall out. Your mother had the power to turn a man against his own hair.

"Someone named Missy Bindle called," she says. "Is she a friend of yours?" The question is ridiculous. Maybe there will be friends again, some time in the future.

Missy Bindle is the mother of the child on whose scalp the problem originally arrived at school, and she's an expert on lice now. She can often be seen holding impromptu informational sessions—outside the school at pick-up time, at the swimming pool in the afternoons, on the street downtown. Lice is never far from her mind, though Lisbet's been clean at least two months. Missy Bindle is starting to seem like one of those old guys who never got over the War.

"There's anecdotal evidence that shampooing prophylactically with Head and Shoulders twice a week is an effective deterrent," she says at the swimming pool, where the mothers have gathered, as if to an oracle.

"You have to buy a metal comb; those plastic ones are no good."

"Vinegar loosens the nits from the hair shaft, but it also interferes with the killing effects of the products."

"Clean hair repels them."

"I heard the opposite," one of the other mothers says. "That slightly dirty hair keeps them away."

You didn't have the heart to tell Missy Bindle what you'd read about the neutralizing property of chlorine on Nix. All the little girls were swimming happily. "Why don't they just drown?" Ariadne asked you. "Why can't I just hold my head under water for five or six hours?" she asked one night when you started crying as you combed.

Did you ever think of this? If your mother gets lice, you are the one who's going to have to go through her hair.

She uses up all the shampoo, disregards the package instructions, shampoos several times in a row. You pray for them to obediently die. When she comes out with her head in a towel, you look at her blankly. If you asked, anyone would tell you: you have to do it. Your undutifulness has never been thrown at you quite so baldly before; you have definitely begun to feel something like awe at the power of these tiny bugs to bring the ugly heart of a thing to light.

You have to hand it to her, though. After she is combed, she does the laundry—yours, Gary's, Ariadne's, even the boyfriend's. She offers to comb Ariadne the next night, but then gets too drunk to do it. But every day till the end of her stay, she does the laundry; she vacuums. She gives up asking careful veiled questions, the meaning of which is, "How could this have happened?" She only says, "*You* kids never had lice" once; seeing your dangerous look, she changes her nuance in mid-stream: "Hmm, I wonder why."

She also can't wait to get out of there. She's got a side trip planned. The day before she goes, she offers to comb your hair, but when you let her, she just ruffles her fingers around your scalp randomly, asking, "Is this one? Is this one? Is *this* one?"

"Never mind," you tell her. Tomorrow you will call the health center, get an answer to the question you forgot to ask last time: "Who combs the parents' hair?"

WHO WILL COMB YOUR HAIR?

Like your own death, this is something you should plan for before it happens. So that you don't have to find yourself sitting on the floor at eleven o'clock on a work night, feeling like a despairing princess in a fairy tale. Many have tried and failed. As a last resort, you've asked your boyfriend, but he fails, too. "Your hair's so overwehelming," he says. He keeps stopping his random, halfhearted combing to argue with you.

"Can't you at least fight and comb at the same time?" you say. Your butt's numb, your eyes ache from two hours of work on Ariadne's head and another hour on his.

"That's it," he says, and he wings the comb across the room. It hits the wall and its little plastic magnifying glass flies off. You begin to cry. You cry for one minute, then you get the phone book and the phone. This is the order: almost-ex-husband, mother, boyfriend, ex-husband's recently jilted girlfriend.

> —strongly recommend trying to avoid getting in situation of having almost-ex-husband's recently jilted girlfriend be last-resort comber

Even if she asks repeatedly; even if she calls before anyone else knows you have them and says, "I've been there; it's awful. Let me know if there's anything I can do to help." Her daughter and Ariadne are in the same class, and Elinor's case of lice seems to be indomitable. Every night, according to Lynette, the girlfriend, Elinor's short, straggly hair is combed till "there's not one speck of anything in it," and every day she is sent home by the school nurse. "They must be jumping on her head from the other children," Lynette says. She starts calling every day. "I know how hard it can be to get someone to comb you out," she says. "Why don't we just set up a time?"

What if you can't avoid it? What if the momentum of lice is giving your life a shape you can only watch transmogrify grotesquely, while your real dreams and aspirations—sitting down to a well-prepared meal without a stomachache, having fifteen minutes left at the end of the day to take a bath or fold laundry—seem to have evaporated with a cold, hard finality?

Under such circumstances, you might find yourself, on a Saturday night, sitting in the bright, overdecorated living room of your almost-ex-husband's recently jilted girlfriend, having a conversation with him in your head. Cute like her, you say, about the room. You are focusing on the enormous cabbage roses on Lynette's living room rug, on the two sweating, warming beers you brought, which are sitting, small in the distance, on the kitchen counter beyond the wide double door.

You know before her finger even touches the stereo's power button that you'll be listening to Jonathon Richman or African dance music. Gary's cassette player's been broken for two years, about the same amount of time as your marriage, so he brings his CDs over to your apartment for the boyfriend to record. You don't tell Lynette that there are at least three other women with the exact microcollection she's now asking you to choose from. Or that the last time Gary went out with her, you asked him, "Did she wear her little headband?" and that Gary laughed and answered, "I'm afraid so."

And she hasn't said to you yet—woman to woman, friend to friend—the comb firmly set in your head, "I *told* Gary he wasn't your father and he didn't have to take care of you." She hasn't yet said, referring to your furniture that you couldn't stand to take because Ariadne hates anything to change: "Look at his *house*. Look at his *stuff*. Look at the way he lives!" She also hasn't said the thing that causes you to wrinkle your eyebrows at its incomprehensibility: "I really hope Ariadne didn't get lice from Elinor. She had them the day Ariadne came over to play, but I didn't tell Gary because I was so mad at him."

She spreads a sheet on the floor to collect the vermin that will be raining from you; she has you sit at her feet, and she puts her small, feathery hands in your hair.

"I think I'm going to write a guide," she says. For other parents, about how to get rid of lice. "Straight talk," Lynette says firmly. You wonder what other kind she thinks she's capable of.

Missy Bindle's writing a guide, too. Why does everyone else have the good ideas? Not that you could ever write a guide, but if you did, maybe it would be something besides straight talk. The more peripheral issues, like: What if lice is the anti-missing-puzzle-piece, the thing that sends all the little pieces of your life flying irretrievably in different directions? Or if it's like secret-tarnish remover—if getting lice is the thing that rubs all the accumulated grime, the obscuring effect of everyday life, off the secrets that have been sitting there forever: you might never be able to forgive your mother, even if you try; you are a better mother than you ever thought you would be and aren't quite sure what to do with that knowledge; you might never be ready for this divorce, even though you know it's a good idea; and another man is not the answer. What to do then. Maybe that would be a guide people could use—not like Missy's or Lynette's, but one for after they get rid of lice. Because—they can't know until it happens, but you know, now—life will never be the same.

One of the ironies of lice is that Gary's the only one who doesn't get them. The hub of infestation, and he remains untouched. Probably it's because he's balding fast, but you have a moment of thinking maybe it's his attitude. He doesn't let anyone close; maybe the lice respect that.

One day Gary feels dizzy and short of breath on the tennis court. He calls to tell you about it. "Get to the doctor," you tell him, which, uncharacteristically, he does. The doctor says he's fine. You have a combing scheduled with him for the next day. "Come at four o'clock," he says. He's found he prefers to comb in natural light, in the late afternoon, in a white plastic chair on the front porch. The combee sits in a child-sized chair in front of him. "I've actually gotten sort of into this," he says.

"You know my little heart attack yesterday?" Gary says. His hands have gotten much better in your hair—quick, firm and decisive.

"My preferred method," he says when you yelp—when he finds a hair shaft with a nit on it, he yanks it clean out of your head. You just let him. You think, maybe lice was the moment your marriage was always waiting for.

"Yeah?" you say. You were just in the middle of talking about the usual things: Ariadne's schedule, her activities sign-up deadlines, which lunch box is at whose house.

"Well, I just thought I'd go through this real quick, in case anything happens to me," he says, and he tells you the provisions of his life insurance policy and Ariadne's college fund, and what to do about the mortgages, and where all the papers are to be found.

"Gary!" You don't need this in the middle of everything.

"Well," he replies.

"Don't die," you tell him, and you don't even mean because then there won't be anybody to comb my hair, or maybe you do.

Your mother is calling every couple of days, asking after everyone's head, trying to hide the fact that she is so glad to be out of there.

"How're you holding up, sweetie?" she asks, and you think about how you will probably die without knowing why words like that make you feel like long fingers are raking your insides, trying to rearrange things in there, screw up the order things have finally fallen into.

"Fine," you say, not mentioning that Ariadne still has lice and Gary has gone to Tulsa to visit his new girlfriend, someone he met at a conference in some other, grown-up world where lice don't circulate. The visit was arranged before the lice trouble; you thought of asking him to change his plans, but you didn't. You were surprised by the knowledge that cornered you: you can't afford—not just yet—to risk hearing Gary say the one thing he never says to you, the thing, like the last louse left on a ravaged scalp, after which, having been rooted out, everything will change and the rest of life will begin.

"Go," you said to him. "Have a good time." You felt utterly abandoned; of course you don't tell your mother that, and you don't tell her this: you've started to see her around.

All your adult life you've dreamed her: walking down the street, unaware that you've caught her, living in your town and not even letting you know. But lately these apparitions have stepped out of your dreams and into real life. You keep seeing her driving around town. Why haven't you ever noticed before how many middle-aged women there are in the world who look exactly like your mother, driving blue Accords? They never see you, and you turn away; you don't want to be seen.

Anyway, if you write a guide, put this in it. The next time one of those women drives by, don't be afraid if something happens. If one of those women in a blue Honda drives by, and you suddenly get a mental picture, almost as if she's bumped you with a fender and caused it to pop out—a picture of you—don't be afraid to look at it.

You might consider using illustrations in the guide. Not just the usual, a magnified picture of a louse with its actual dimensions and Latin name written underneath it, but maybe something more like this: a surprised woman, standing on the sidewalk watching another woman who's not her mother drive by. You might need a series of illustrations to show this. Her problem has reached monumental proportions, though it's still invisible to the outside world, and she is just about to decide to take desperate measures—beg for a prescription for the really poisonous stuff, send away for information about home schooling, shave her head and her child's head, set fire to all their possessions and move away to the desert—*do what she has to do*—when the problem suddenly, miraculously, eradicates itself. Not gradually, like it's supposed to—the dead bugs falling out, the tiny eggs prised from the hair shafts over hours and days with the little comb, the methodical correcting of the problem over time, which, everyone will tell you, is the one and only way you will ever be able to crawl back into your life—but all in a single, stunning instant. Hundreds, thousands of the little things jump off her head, like

—Medusa with detached snakes
—Sea monkey party
—Cartoon sweat beads
—A bunch of happy olden-days kids (Missy Bindle says post-1970s rise in lice due to DDT ban) jumping out of trees, yelling a thousand little "Geronimo"s

leaving her like she was before (nothing like she was before?): a little light-headed, a little uninhabited, a little able to feel, whenever anyone mentions it (—ask Leon: can he draw this?) the absent itch.

Stephanie Rosenfeld lives in Salt Lake City where she works as a pastry chef. She's published stories previously in *Other Voices* and *Cream City Review*.

"And that's our plan. Any questions?"

TAD LINCOLN'S LADDER OF DREAMS/
Emily Pease

IF SHE HELD SÉANCES, then you can understand it, there were so many deaths. How she watched her little boy die. How her eyes turned to the small shallow spot in the bed—his ghost—when they finally lifted him away from the sheets. Feverish boy, with wet brown hair, glassy-eyed. She had wiped his brow. Had held his small hand and caressed each small finger, lifting them at the knuckles. Laid her head on his chest, his tender ribs, to hear his dying heart. In the upstairs room a window had been opened. Rain puddled on the sill. The boy's cat stepped its quiet paws over the floor, rubbed its back against the bed, crouched to jump—its back legs tight, ready to spring—while the boy lay in his dark fever. But she lunged at the cat, kicking her stiff black shoe at its head, so terrified had she become that her boy would be robbed of his last tiny breath.

Someone had to take him, and it would not be she. Neighbors came, and the doctor. And when they finally carried him away, wrapped like a doll in winding sheets, she fell against the wall and wept. This was the beginning of her long sorrow.

Little Eddy Lincoln, age three, rest in peace.

His father wrote him a poem. In the light of a single candle, beneath rings of shadows, he bent over the paper and thought of the whole delicateness of the world, its vapors and mysteries. What it had been like when he was just a boy of nine in the wilderness in spring, when the grasses grow green again and the buds split a branch open at its tip. What it had been like to be left alone there, with owls screeching in the night. So he remembered his mother's death. How she groaned in the loft of the one-room house, inches away from where he slept. Where she had gone he could not be sure, though at times he would see her in his dreams, the pale Nancy.

But his tiny boy—now he was in heaven, certainly. *For of such is the kingdom of God.* He had the stonemason carve it in white marble for the grave.

These are the stories you do not know. How the young father rode his horse into the forest, thinking of spirits. How he thought he heard his mother's thin voice—believed he saw her there, near a sapling oak—and then, as if the world were controlled by ghosts, felt at once that she was gone, felt this utterly, the way he now felt his little boy's death. How he looked out into the blurred space in front of him and heard the small sound of Eddy Lincoln's cry, and all the cries of the dead. God gave, he thought, extravagantly. Gave the tenderness of a baby's hands, a baby's slight breath on the cheek. Gave this land, and these trees, and these flickering shadows on the leaves of the trees. And then let it die. And if God had let his young mother die back in the wilderness, before he, her boy, had ever considered her to be separate from himself—and if he could then let his tiny boy die after fifty-two days of fever—then he could die also—soon—overnight, when he was not ready. And he would join them in the other world.

And Mother. She walked into the baby's room, then walked out, then walked in—averting her eyes, trying not to see the bed where Eddy had died. The wood floors were silent. The bed was smooth. In a corner, as if they had been swept there, lay the empty shoes of her second baby.

Which sent her into the darkest despair. She would make herself sick with grief, they said. All things die, they said; you must accept this. But still, she wanted to know: If God gives life, then why take it back?

She turned to her one living son, the older son, a boy of six, chin and eyes like hers. She pulled him to her side and clung to his waist, but already his look had grown distant, since he now knew death, and since he felt, though he could not express it, the desperation in her fingers.

Then Willie was born. No one would call him a replacement—she would not, ever—but the brown eyes were familiar. The seasons changed. And the father felt, as he heard this new baby cry, that he had been to death and back.

Then I was born—Thomas, after Thomas Lincoln, the tall, haggard, rough farmer and opportunist, my grandfather. When his wife died in her bed, leaving him in the forest, alone with two children, a cow, a horse, soil bled of substance—what words came to him as he buckled the leather halter on the horse and rode away, leaving the children by themselves? The boy Abraham had watched him disappear into the trees, and he had watched in wonder when his father appeared again, weeks later, after rains and long black nights abandoned, with a wagon and another horse and carved furniture and more children and a new wife.

The old man faded into the past, away on an Indiana farmstead, eyes fixed on the weather. But in his name I came to be, the last son, and with a cleft lip I spoke muddled, twisted words that caused my father to laugh and draw me to him, his big hands lifting.

But Willie was his other self.

Another story you do not know: how Willie had Abraham Lincoln's eyes, and his lean height (he would have been tall), and his keen wisdom. How as we grew older, he was the favorite, the one who wrote poems and spoke in a gentle voice, with light in his face. Mother looked at him and felt the quick bright flame of fear—*if he should die!* She heard him speak and thought she heard the voice of an angel, and as she crossed the room where I slept with him, she looked at his rumpled clothes and his stockings on the floor, and thought how full it all seemed, and how passable.

If she held séances, then you can understand it.

On the morning he left for the White House, my father stepped out into the street. It was raining, and the sky hung white and cold and distant. But the people were jubilant; they lifted their hats, they called, Speech! Speech! I heard my father's laugh, but they did not hear it, he stood so quiet and still. They drew in, shuffling, damp, and he lingered, for a moment appearing almost as if he would reach out his arm and bless them, he was so solitary. He began to speak, and they hushed. It was a sad day, he said, to be leaving his beloved town and all his beloved friends, and he did not know when, or whether, he would return. His voice was high and strange. I stood near him, my gaze on his veined hands, and I thought that if I could, I would crawl beneath his long coat and cling to the drape of his trousers and his lean, hard legs. He boarded the train. The smoke from the engine rose in thick white clouds, floating back, and the big steel wheels turned slowly in the rails, clattering. My father leaned from the platform at the back and waved. A banner rippled at his feet and he smiled, but to me, his eyes looked stunned, and as the train pulled away, he stood there still, like rock.

Imagine a country so huge it seems to stretch from pole to pole, broad and flat, with deserts and plains and rivers. Imagine a country yet to be charted, on a map marked only with the regular grid of latitude and longitude and the snaking, wavering lines of rivers. For two weeks, the train moved slowly over that land while my father watched from the windows. In his mind, the country was full of strangers. He saw their eager, grimacing faces, and he was afraid. There was talk that he would be killed. Someone suggested a disguise. Move away from the windows, they said, sit within.

He looked out from the train and remembered the feel of the Sangamon River as it rose beneath his flatboat. How he stood near the edge of the boat, with the water lapping at his feet, and pushed a pole into the muddy bottom. The boat slipped across the surface like a fly; the water slapped against the boards. He rode on the train and thought of the depths of the river and the long, stretching waves the flatboat made. On his way to Washington, to the edge of the country, he looked out from the train and thought of water.

They said he would be safer if he had children by his side. Mother packed us for the trip on the racing train behind his train, dressing us like little men in suits, and then she watched as her trunks were lifted into the cars. She stood in the freezing mist, solemn, like a queen. She took my hand. Willie leaned into her skirts. I am now to be Madame President, she said, and you will be the president's sons.

We reached his train in Indianapolis—the presidential cars, shining orange and black, with flags and festoons—and the crowds pushed in. The little silk rim of Mother's hat lifted in a breeze, and she turned me loose. Someone in the crowd shouted, Show us the boys! and I heard her voice, like a coo. Here, she said, taking me up, and Willie . . . We looked out at the people, watched the cold vapor rise from their mouths. A man called out, The little presidents! and Mother pushed us forward in the direction of the train. Then *he* emerged, lowering his head beneath the doorway of the train car, then standing, straight as a tree, his hair tousled as if he had been sleeping. He peered long into the faces, caught sight of Mother and smiled broadly, his eyes bright as glass. She tugged my hand, squeezing with her soft glove, and we went to him, not knowing then that we were his protection, his careless small bodyguards against whom no man would charge.

In the great cavern of the White House, Mother wandered from room to room. The gas flames wavered in the sconces on the walls; the lights rose in halos. Her eyes scanned the molding and the windows; she pressed her thumbs against the wallpapering, tested the brass knobs on the doors. In the Blue Room, her fingers trailed languidly across the chairs, where she felt for dust and in the pantry she turned out the cupboards, taking down china plates and teacups, pitchers, bowls and platters—service to Washington and Adams and Jefferson that was no longer good enough, she said, since it was old and full of ghosts.

She took us on her long trips, and we ran like monkeys, crawling beneath the seats in the trains and racing in the aisles. At Baltimore, we were taken from the train and ushered to a coach, to be safe. Soldiers watched us, stiff shouldered and grim. We took the quiet roads through the forests, in secret, like runaways, Mother fanning the dust, talking constantly. It was fine furniture she was after, and carpeting, and mirrors made of new silver. She wanted to stand in the shimmer of those mirrors and admire her own reflection, her broad skirts swaying softly, as if by enchantment. We rode with her to the stores, to William H. Carryl & Bro., Humphrey & Co. and John Alexander's, passing unnoticed through the streets, where soldiers gathered in new regiments, marching south. Later, when we returned to Washington, wagons pulled up behind the mansion each morning. Men brought crates and unloaded them into the halls, and then they unrolled giant woven mats over the floors, and painted floor cloths, and thick carpets the color of the sea.

One room Mother made entirely purple and gold, and then a bed was brought in, and a marble washstand, and a center table figured in rosewood. The bed was big enough for a giant, with drapes of purple silk and gold tassels; Willie and I climbed into the pillows and pretended we were kings.

In the rooms down below us, the people came. They stepped through the portico and walked the halls, wandering, looking for the president. They stood in lines, held papers, took biscuits from their pockets and ate, crumbling them in their nervous fingers. They thought they would see a god, but it would just be him—our father—and what could he do? A soldier needed to be brought home, one woman told him—her husband had died and she could not take care of the farm alone.

(Another thing you do not know: how my father loved the company of men, their tales, their laughter; how he went to Harvard to see our older brother, Robert—sat in his room with all the boys, listening to them play the banjo and sing. Or how he became like a father to young Elmer Ellsworth, who rode with him on the train to the White House— and how he took in other young men, John Nicolay and John Hay, like sons or brothers. Ellsworth slept in the White House like my father's own boy; he paraded about, made plans; he put on fancy trousers and a sash and called himself a Zouave. My father called him "Colonel," let him gather a whole regiment of Zouaves like himself, zealous, wild, turning somersaults by the hundreds on the lawn outside. Ellsworth would go to take Alexandria, seize the town in the foggy dawn, but when he reached the town and climbed to take a rebel flag, he was shot. They brought the body to my father, and he dropped his face into his big hands and wept. Mother made Ellsworth a wreath of flowers, and for three days, his coffin lay down the hall, where Willie and I refused to creep.)

In the afternoons, we rode a pony in front of the White House, trotted past the people as they filed inside. Want to see Old Abe? I taunted them. He's over there, I said, way over there. I pointed to the street, to the farthest building, to the horizon beyond Washington, and they squinted with doubting eyes. It was a broad, muddy town. We could smell the river. Gulls flew overhead. Inside the house, we could swing the brass spigots on the walls and watch river water spill into the pretty basins. In winter, the water was so cold it was flaked with dirty ice, but it was muddy warm in the summer. We leaned over a basin and put our hands in, palms and fingers up, watching the water pour down, hoping to see tadpoles fall, like salmon in a stream.

He thought constantly of war. A guard sat in the hall beside the door of his office; over his desk, Andrew Jackson looked down from the wall. They said he must be careful, that he was a target, but he shrugged. If they will kill me, they will kill me, he insisted, I cannot stop them. At night, in the oval room where we played, he told his dreams, how a hazy white boat took him over the water, rushing across the rippling surface so swiftly he had no time to be afraid. Then he lifted us on his knees. I wonder, he said, how Old Bob is doing? I wonder if that old horse misses me. Do you think? And our dog—does he think of us now that we have gone and left him in Illinois? And our cow, he said, laughing. When we go home again, we will have Old Bob back, and Fido, and the cow.

He let us keep goats, Nanny and Nanko, and we hitched one to a chair. Willie and I and our friends, Bud and Holly and Julia, hitched up the goat and let her pull the chair through the East Room as if it were a carriage, running with her knobby head bent low, twisting her neck, pushing the waiting people aside. At night I liked to take my little goat to bed. Father would come into our room to undress us, laying me down like a baby to pull my trousers over my legs and feet. The goat cried, and he said he now had three babies in the room, but only one had a taste for linen. Be careful while you sleep, he said, she will nibble you naked. Then he lay with us in the darkness, his long arms stretching across the bed, and Willie said prayers aloud, his high voice filling the room like song.

But on stormy nights, when lightning pierced the lace in the windows, Mother would cry out from her darkened room—Father!—and then we would hear him rise, hear his footsteps on the carpet as he slipped through the high door to her chamber. He talked to her calmly—but to us, her nightmares made the house terror-filled, cavernous, horrible. While she cried, we lay in the darkness holding hands. By then we knew every face in the house, every bust, every portrait. In the Blue Room, George Washington stood in his perpetual pose, the quick lightning blazing his white hair, and in the attic where we liked to play, white visitors' cards with their inky scripted names—ghosts, all of them—lay scattered over the floor like snow. What made her scream? What hallucinations? During the afternoons she complained of pain at her temple, beating, she said, like a drum, and so she grew angry, and her eyes flamed, and lines formed around her mouth. She took medicine from a bottle and grew quiet, slept on her bed with her back against the pillows, curled like a cat. Then, when she was no longer sick, she drove through the city to make her purchases: hats, shoes, hosiery, lace, jewelry, dresses, and hundreds and hundreds of fine little gloves.

She would be queen of the land, the First Lady, so she held a great party, with five hundred guests and the marine band playing "The Mary Lincoln Polka." There were long decorated tables with hams and roasted turkeys and pheasants, fruits and breads—and in the center, a miniature Fort Sumter built of glazed white sugar, glistening in the glow of the high chandeliers. Women watched her sweep about the room in her white silk dress, massive, with its long train and black flowers sewn over all, like daisies in a meadow. Her high, loud voice lifted over the crowd, and her laughter rang out, incessant until far into the deep night, two o'clock, three o'clock, four o'clock—while upstairs I lay in a fever, monsters in my dreams, and Willie, too, lay limp in the great purple bed. The band played below us, and I heard cymbals in my sleep; the people danced, they chattered and their voices marched. Mother came, leaned over my bed, kissed my cheeks, and I felt her wet, warm tears. And then Father, too, holding my hand . . . and then the daylight came, and the afternoon, and the evening, and another day, and I could not go down the hall to see Willie, I was so weak, the chill of typhus in my limbs.

He had asked for Bud to sit by him, and so Bud sat. Mother wiped Willie's brow, over and over, as if by wiping it she could erase the sickness from his body. And Bud sat, tapping his shoes on the floor, leaning against the back of the chair, while death descended like a late-day shadow, dark, transparent, imperceptible to anyone not looking. My father smelled the oncoming death, and Bud, helpless to go, sat long in the chair beside his friend's bed and let the shadow fall. At the last hour, they say, Willie rose on his pillow and talked brightly of a sudden—Bud! he said, remember the time we . . . ?

When Willie did not breathe again, my father's long shoulders fell and he wept, leaving his boy still in the purple silk and gold lace. He was too good, he said, for this earth. Then he came to the room where I lay, the fever slipping from me, the light returning to my eyes, and he grasped my arm. Now you cannot leave us too, he said, pleading, and the grief was so dark in his face that I knew Willie was gone forever.

In her room, Mother screamed and rolled on the floor as if she had turned mad. Who is God, she said, but the devil? To have taken Willie in his perfection, to have stilled his warm, strong heart. She closed her eyes and saw his face, his dark brown eyes, his lips open in sleep. This cannot be! she said—it will not, she insisted—and so she ordered dresses made only of black, with black lace and ribbons, and she pulled a filmy black veil over her eyes and made herself into a ghost. Then she called Willie's name. In the oval room, with the dark bookcases surrounding her, she sat still as stone and waited to see his face appear in the air: Willie, back from the dead, half alive, like the spirits already in the house, restless in the wisp of history. Willie, Willie, she called in the darkened room, holding hands with the grim necromancers she had summoned by day. They bowed their heads, listening for the sounds of the dead, and they tilted their chins upward, watching for whatever might appear up above, certain that when they saw it, they would recognize the celestial shapes of Willie and Eddy.

The curtains were drawn. Down below, the people came in their long, shuffling lines, packing scissors in their pockets, and knives. With furtive hands they sliced medallions from the lace curtains and dropped them into their bags. They knelt shamelessly and cut ragged swatches from the Brussels carpets, leaving threads loose on the boards like chaff. Late at night, if she ventured there, Mother stepped into the holes and shrugged bitterly. Everywhere there were signs of the dead. If the curtains were mangled, then it was death that had done the deed: the holes would remain.

He slipped out at midnight, breathing the dewy air, and walked across the lawn, grass wet as a meadow. In the sky, he thought he saw lightning, although there were stars. On the day he had buried Willie, a northeast wind had come in, dashing the city with thick, gray rain. He'd pulled a shawl over his shoulders and ridden behind the caisson, his eyes on Willie's small black coffin; later he watched, stunned, as the coffin was lifted into the rainy tomb.

Now he walked in the night to hear news from the war. Across the lawn, in a clean bare room at the War Department, a telegraph tapped out battle reports. He took the papers in his hands, and his mind filled with pictures of the dead: boys in vast farm fields, their dead eyes wide, leaning like gray dolls against fences. With a hollow heart he remembered Willie.

Another story you do not know: How he went with Mother to her séances and watched her wait, breathlessly, for her sons to appear. How he followed, reluctantly, up the great stairs to the upper chambers where a candle would be lit—followed the quaking mediums, with their mysterious satchels and shawls, up the stairs to meet with the dead. Should he tell them of his dreams? The boat on the wide, silver sea? Should he tell them how often its bow pierced the surface of the water at such great speed, taking him to the unknown shore? The two faces in the mirror—that dream—should he tell them? All the world was full of dreams, he thought. And while the living dreamed, the dead were . . . where, he could not say.

He wondered: If the dead would return simply by asking them, then would not the whole country be calling in the night, rapt and expectant in the smoky light of candles—and would not the dead then come? All the fallen soldiers, North and South, and all the dead children, Willie and Eddy, would they not then appear, in misty reunion, to comfort the living? He followed Mother, weary, full of dread, and as he walked, he heard the old stairs crack beneath his feet.

In such a house, I could not sleep. As the windows grew dark and the flames rose in the lamps, I stayed with my father, wandering in his footsteps. I had no one else. Mother had grown distant and gloomy. She would not have children in the house, she said, since they reminded her of Willie. So Bud did not come again, or Holly, or Julia. Only the generals came, and the other men. They sat at the big table in my father's office, and I played beneath them, watching their shoes. When they left, I lay on the floor and studied the ceiling, or else I stood at the windows to see the trees sway across the face of the moon. The nights dragged onward, silence thundering in my ears, until at last Father would carry me, my legs wrapped around his waist, to his room.

We slept together—Abraham Lincoln and I, his last little boy—clinging in the night as if a flood would rise beneath us and carry us away. In the bed where we lay, I looked out into the room and felt the ceiling closing over us like a veil. I rolled onto my side; I touched a knee to my father's cool, prickling leg. Against his long body, I felt small as an egg, smooth and white, and as I drifted into sleep I felt myself recede into the hollow of his arms.

But on the nights when he did not sleep so well, I awoke to hear my father talking, steady and pleading. He squirmed, more animal than man, with his black hair standing straight up from his scalp and his heavy, pouched eyes closed tight. He pulled me to him with one hand, and he quivered. What did he dream? In his mind he saw red flames in Indiana, perhaps, from the fire he had built with his own young hands, or he heard turkeys pounding in the brush. Soldiers and horses. Cannon fire. His wife's cry.

I was too young to pity him. Instead, I saw him look at me in the mornings, when the sunlight paled the windows, and I felt grateful. If to make himself live he needed me with him, then I was willing, following him like a shadow, a little Abraham, his charm. And so we arose, stretching from our tangled sleep, and he dressed me, folding his knees and squatting on the floor to button me up. Tad Lincoln, they said: look at how he takes him everywhere—the president and his boy.

We rode in a carriage to see the troops; we took a trip on the river. He laid a hand on my shoulder and showed me how the paddle wheels rolled, how the water's depth matched the curve of the shoreline, and he told stories of poling flatboats heavy with the weight of snorting, stinking pigs. We went to the theaters and sat high above the stage, watching the actors come in from the wings, and then in the White House I got my own stage, with stairs and a curtain and a dressing room in back, and I made shows, and he came, my best patron. And still the war went on, and Father grew older, his body becoming brittle, while Mother, dressed in black, kept to herself, bringing friends— doting, hungry men—to sit with her in the Red Room at night.

Some mornings she left the house laden with boxes, her black bonnet tied tight below her chin. At the hospitals then she would walk among the beds, bringing cakes to the wounded soldiers. It is as if I am visiting my own sons, she said, and Father agreed—all have suffered, he said, we cannot overestimate our loss. Still the nights wore long, and Mother whimpered in her sleep: There is a rapping on the wall, she cried, and I know it is Willie. Father looked stricken. He took a Bible from a shelf, pointed to an open page, to Jacob's story: *". . . and he took of the stones of that place, and put them for his pillows, and lay down in that place to sleep. And he dreamed, and behold a ladder set up on the earth, and the top of it touched to heaven: and behold the angels of God ascending and descending. . . ."*

Then he told his own dream, a new one: how he had risen from his bed in the night and walked through the White House, the sound of weeping in the halls. How he had risen from his bed and walked, though he did not feel his feet on the floor, and then, turning a corner, he saw it—the funeral bier, the coffin, the guards. In his dream he asked, Who has died? And a soldier answered: The president.

He held the Bible in his hands. I watched his ragged face. In all our slumbering nights, I could not remember his rising from the bed, could not remember the feel of his arms and hands pressing into the mattress as he stood, bare feet on the floor, leaving me in the shallow spot where he had slept by my side. It did not happen, I told him—it was only a dream, but by then he had turned to look out the window, and it seemed to me that he could see for miles.

But he could not see Booth.

The war was over; there was cannon fire in the streets. On Good Friday, church bells rang at noon. Mother prepared herself for the theater, chattering brightly in a striped dress, and then Father took her by the arm. As I watched them go, I thought the world had never smelled so sweet, the air so damp and clean, so full of lilacs and honeysuckle and crickets in the grass.

For a while I stood by myself on the portico and watched the carriages roll down Pennsylvania Avenue, the men riding horses and the soldiers returning from the war. Then it was my time to go to the theater, to the National, where we got seats in the front, my tutor and I, to see *Aladdin*. Musicians played clarinets and shook tambourines, and in a puffy cloud of smoke a genie appeared, saving poor Aladdin, while over at Ford's my father took Mother's hand, squeezing it, and she leaned against his shoulder in their high, decorated box above the stage.

And someone rushed down the aisle, and the actors on the stage looked out into the lights with puzzled faces. A man leaned over, whispering; my tutor took me by the arm and we rose in our seats. The audience made shuffling sounds as I was swept up the aisle in the darkness, my feet almost missing the ground, and then I heard them say it—*he has been shot*—and the tutor bent over me as if to keep me dry from rain, and he pushed me out of the theater and into the street toward home. Later, when midnight came and no one brought my father back, they laid me on his empty bed and removed my shoes. The room was like pitch, and the halls were hushed and vacant. I closed my eyes and felt everything turn. As I lay beneath the arm of Tom Pen, our guard, and heard his unfamiliar breaths, so close to my ear, I knew my father was gone.

There are stories about what happened then—how Booth was pursued, lame and terrified, into Virginia. How, to his surprise, no applauding audience went to greet him, the murdering hero, on the roads. And when he was shot, finally, in the neck, with the barn burning behind him, he died—*asked* to die—on the porch of a man named Garrett. In Washington people crowded into the streets, crying. They filed into the White House to see my father, dead and gray as stone, before he would be taken home at last to Illinois. For a time, all was black and white—his dark face, his white shirt buttoned high beneath his black beard, and the funeral bier, like a four-poster bed, black, with its ceiling of white satin, and the black crepe, hanging like webs over doors and windows.

But on that first morning when they brought him back, dead, to the house, they had gone to the Prince of Wales Room first, stripped him naked and embalmed his body on a table. If I had crept down the hall then, I would have heard the men talking as they worked, heard their solemn, ministering voices through the door. But I did not go down. Instead, I wandered upstairs, room to room, aimless, like an animal trapped in a box, or else I buried my head in the pillows of his bed— our bed—breathing the last faint smells of his slumber.

Mother did not go down, although she knew what they were doing, since Willie had died there, his small body laid out in that same room, with its lavender walls and curtains yellow as marigolds. She had fixed that room with great care, had chosen its rich carpets and its grand, lacy bed. But she would not go there again.

Some say she lost her mind, and it's almost true. At his great funeral, she did not appear. And when they lifted his coffin into the train, placing Willie's small coffin beside it, she did not watch. The train rolled for weeks. In the cities it stopped, and they unloaded the coffin, lifted the lid, allowed people to come see. Along desolate stretches, bonfires burned in the night, the fires of mourning and farewell. From all this, she withdrew. Instead, in her delirium she stayed locked within. Doctors came. They said, We have never seen such grief, she is convulsing. And I wandered, room to room, went out on the roof to see the horses pass by on the streets, and I watched from my high perch to see the little goats graze. Heat rose in waves at midday, and the river smelled of fish. Down below, in all the big rooms, the people came again, bringing their scissors and knives, cutting, carrying away what they could—until at last, Mother opened her door and took me by the hand to go, no longer the son of the president, just a boy.

We boarded a great ship, and we watched America recede from sight. Mother looked long into my face, and I was afraid. She was all I had. She took me to France, to Italy, to Germany, and we lived like refugees, climbing stairs in the afternoons to our meager rooms. Still, she was covered in black, and her cheeks had grown painfully full. She followed me, fluttering her nervous hands before my face, since she could see I was no longer little and would not be caressed.

She took me to a German school, where I stayed with German boys and learned German games and spoke *Deutsch* until I was American no longer; and then she took me to England to teach me English again. I grew tall, but she hardly noticed—and in all my study I lost my lisp, but she did not hear it. In the chill of spring, I fell ill, but she would not believe it.

And so a last story you do not know: how the familiar fever returned, and the restless, suffocating nights, but she refused to see my suffering. We boarded a ship bound for home, and she stood at the rail and looked out over the Atlantic, reaching, as if she could rein in the sea. My skin grew pale and damp, but she could not look. As soon as we get home, she said, you will be strong again. The doctors will help. You will sit in the sun, drink the good water. . . .

But in the night, when she thought I might be dreaming, she crept to the chair where I sat, the air thin in my lungs, and she drew close. She placed a hand on my shoulder, leaning over me with open, desperate eyes, and I knew then that she was memorizing my face. If she held séances, she would want to remember it—my dying face. With her left hand she gripped my knee; she dropped her forehead to my chest. She waited to hear my breath, but all around us there was only the hollow noise of the wind in our ears and the splash of the deep, eternal sea.

Emily Pease is the winner of this year's Editors' Prize in Fiction. She is a student in the MFA program at Warren Wilson College and has published a story in *Witness*.

"Whew! That was close! We almost
decided something!"

DAWN, WITH CARDINALS / *Jeffrey Levine*

After separating from Penelope, Ulysses
takes a smallish cottage out of town,
bounded by deep woods on one side, a golf course
on the other where children sled or startle frogs,
depending on the season.

Crows strut their turf beneath the plum trees,
furl their capes and bob like drunks.
Of the night birds, owls map the taller pines
with their iridescent eyes and moon hens
peck at drops of evening dew.

When the divorce is done, he'll move
to an island some miles out,
where he may settle on a narrow road
beside a spit of sand—beyond that, sea.
He could earn a modest pension
crafting bird feeders from mill scraps,
keep a brace of hunting dogs for company
and rake the silt for clams and oysters at low tide.

For now, he contents himself
recording local bird calls,
but forgets them quickly as he learns, save
the cardinal's song, a slight and mournful chirping
heard each morning just outside his porch.

And always the same two birds—
she quarrelsome, he quiet or detached or maybe
    mystified
at his helplessness to make a difference. Or, cocksure
he does, you see it in the ebony beak, crimson breast.
Look, the birdbath is full of cool clear water and still
she carries on like that, sharp
staccato chirps, high pitched, unwavering.
He with flutters but no sound, something holding on

---

inside him, something faintly chipped.
Not that Ulysses planned to wake so early
every morning. Sometimes you don't believe
in ritual for days or weeks, until it's a proven thing,
but here it is, persistent and regular.

Ulysses lets dawn filter through the screened porch.
First no light, then light.
First no birds, then song.
No wind; wind.

ONE MONTH BEFORE HIS 50TH BIRTHDAY /
Jeffrey Levine

Ulysses took up weighing himself after sex.
Hair wet, arms sore, still he felt it urgent as sleep
after months of sailing or a month of wine,
when home sounded a faint, remembered song,
the men's silk tents engorged with treasure and willing slaves
cordoned a bruised & blooded coast.

Penelope could hear him open the walk-in closet
where he kept the bathroom scale. If the sex was good,
she'd be talking about something,
I don't know. Something about their clifftop house,
what needed doing. About their son, surly
& distant, who seemed to disapprove of her.

Ulysses guessed he might have set
a better example for the boy, but he wouldn't say—
because it seemed obvious, & besides,
he'd be in the walk-in weighing himself.

He'd shower & not think about it anymore—
weight or sons or foreign treasure. Shower
& climb into bed again;
pick up an old crossword puzzle while Penelope
hooked her own robe over her shoulder,
crooked her finger through the loop the way his sailors
held their windbreakers in bleached port towns,

and Ulysses would watch Penelope cross the room,
the bracelets coppered around her wrists,
her face red from sex, still striking in some lights—
this light, morning light—then look away
so she wouldn't catch him staring at the beauty spot
on her left breast, at her square shoulders, her rump.

Below, a black ship laded butts of salted meat
while his wife made the faucet squeak
and steam slipped beneath the bathroom door.

PENELOPE DRAWS FROM LIFE/
Jeffrey Levine

I miss the old simplicity of things,
seashore with boardwalk and a book, not reading.
Evenings with Haydn's quartets,
singing the viola line to myself.
Perhaps I'm just obsessive, the Big Moment
just a moment, nothing more, it comes,
it goes, armor shatters and life goes on. . . .

I give an art class in the fall, Drawing from Life:
where students practice drawing with one eye closed
so their hands invent dimension guided by rhythm only.
But to confuse my charges, I pose as their life model
while speaking about myth and meaning,
and reading pages from my journals as they work
to cover up with charcoal where my bones cleave
to my flesh and my body bends into its sighing.

I spend my nights wondering why Ulysses
would not let me watch him die.
He waited until nearly midnight,
after even the hospice nurse had given in.
Just before I left, he demanded two teaspoons of tea,
two more of wine and another dose of morphine.
Communion for the godless.

When he could no longer speak,
I lifted his transparent hand.
Squeeze mine, I asked, *if you agree to share
what you find out,*
and when I felt a finger tighten—
it was right to go.

IT TURNS OUT CIRCE HAS SOMETHING OF A PAST / *Jeffrey Levine*

Have I told you about the year I danced?
Before we met, in clubs,
I stripped for drunks.
You would think the closeness crushing,
but no one said a word, no one ever
touched me. Was lonely art, like painting
without models, without light.
I was a brilliant tease,
brushed naked note by note until I deepened,
locked to a place with no connection to bar stools,
the shy staring. Sometimes

I stripped in clubs behind private walls in old Miami
where I could conjugate my nakedness:
nudo, nudas, nuda, nudamos, nudan. No
narcissism, this wasn't pumping iron. *Nada,*
it was nothing for me to do it all for them.

You ask why I did not say about the dancing.
One day, a man watched as he spoke
into a telephone smaller than a sparrow.
He took me with him, talked for five days
while I ate and slept and danced for him.
He said his insides had annealed.
He had alloyed his metals.
He spoke like that, the talker in him.

Said he had sucked dry all his pronouns,
had no way to move inside, or press out
against the rock. Called me his cockatiel,
though he didn't get the irony: bird of paradise,
the female, the one without plumage.
Toward the end, I saw my body from above
—no bird—a spotted fish scooped in the net,
quiet, quivering and glazed.

TELEMACHOS IN SAN MIGUEL /
Jeffrey Levine

My midnight over, in which no burnt incense,
no scented arms no ankle bells. Neither hookah nor adagio
nor windows shut against the prying moon,
yet windows anyway, courtyard below, its scattering
of pulque pots and Spanish tile in ochre, burnt sienna;
and Mexican hands sewing something yellow
in the lightless morning, stitching closed
this night with raveled flax.

While close in the creel fresh fish red and scaly,
fish with Indian names, names like chanting—
hua-chi-nan-go, gilled god of the shallow waters, god of scales—
Then, to what use each month below my window
fishmongers send another virgin, and who am I
to put an end to this?

One carries the god scaled god with olives
roasted over the fire pan—"For you,"—"usted"—
the formal one, the "you" between children
and their elders or servants and their lords.
Don so-and-so, "For you," she says, and lets me shy
her hands above that black-maned head
the way what other earthbound god could want?

As if she knows no better, better
merchants come here as they come,
carting fish and virgins, Madonnas sewing
and Madonnas with their red-scaled sons of gods.
They know, and still weave morning in this courtyard
of ochre tile and greenless vines below my windows,
skyless dawn above—
charred fish for water, tears for salt.

Jeffrey Levine is the winner of this year's Larry Levis Editors' Prize. He's published poems previously in a number of magazines.

HEP-LOCK/*Adria Bernardi*

A YEAR AFTER I HAVE been back on my feet, sleep deprived with a baby, I am watching television. I am laughing hard. Frazier and his father, Martin, are bickering as they reluctantly enter a hospital room. They tiptoe gingerly, comedic, bumbling, bumping into each other, not wanting to enter. I hope we're not disturbing you, they say to the patient. This takes me back.

But what grabs me by the shoulders and shakes me hard is the sight of the hospital bed, the way that it folds at the waist. There is instant recall of plastic sliding beneath the bedsheet, of the bedsheets twisted and askew by the end of the day and the foot of the bed left uncovered. Recall of how I fumbled to locate the remote that moved the mattress up and down. The way the thick white plastic cord would be draped over the bed rail, only to drop to the floor, dangling below, wedged between nightstand and bed. I would try to fish it out, reel the cord back in, and it would snag on a corner somewhere I could not see. And I, in my massive state, would roll over to try to recover it, yanking, or, if that didn't work, getting up from bed so that I could squat down, reach under the bed, grope for it, only to have a nurse walk in and ask, What is it you're looking for?

Isn't it good that these details are not readily available? It means I have gotten past it. I am saying right off, there was a good outcome. Four-fifteen A.M., Friday, November 19. Four pounds, twelve ounces. A boy.

They whisk me in, don't make me wait in the waiting room. This should be a warning.

Then I am sitting on a chair next to a desk, and the nurse-midwife is dipping a thin strip of paper into a plastic cup. She says there is a high level of protein in my urine. As she says this, I am thinking, we will certainly have to keep an eye on that.

As soon as I give my consent to see a doctor, I am taken across the hallway, and a doctor is there waiting. *A doctor is there waiting.* This should also be a warning—doctors do not wait—but I do not sense this signal, except for a very remote light in the back of my head, which I extinguish each time it blinks. My coat is draped over my arm; I'm ready to go home now, resolved to rest more. The doctor explains the situation to me. She doesn't say: You're not leaving. She says: We would like to keep you in the hospital for observation. I deliberate; I have a choice, yet as soon as I say yes, the forms appear instantaneously. Poof. From thin air. The nurse-midwife says she'll walk the paperwork through the hospital for me. I am flattered by all the attention, amazed that everyone is so considerate.

Everything is fine, but they're putting me into the hospital for observation, I say to my husband over the phone, trying to minimize his alarm. I am oh-so-even-keeled.

The baby would come late; that is what I have prepared myself for so I will not become impatient and anxious at the end. I was going to swim right up until the day before birth, walk, be a good, strong woman, give natural birth. Suddenly we speak of *viability*, a baby whose lungs might not be sufficiently developed, so that I will be getting shots of steroids. Once in the right hip, and six hours later in the left. A week later, provided the baby has not come, I will get another round.

I am not prepared for this new vocabulary: *Proteinuria. Betamethasone.*

Enormous, I clamber into the hospital bed, which is astoundingly high off the ground. A nurse tells me, don't watch TV. The flashing light will trigger eye movement, she says, which will stimulate you and tire you out. I decide she is an alarmist.

The baby inside is measured in grams. Eleven hundred. What does this mean? Maybe a respirator but probably not. The baby looks good; it would probably do very well, the attending resident says. You mean, I might have the baby now? It's October and the due date is Christmas. A cesarean section? Wait, let's go back a minute. Two weeks ago, I was hiking up a very steep hill in the province of Quebec, on a trail that led to a breathtaking view of the Saguenay Fjord, short of breath but pushing on, and now you say the baby might have to come out today? Or that I could be lying on my left side for the next two months?

Why are my eyes moist? he wants to know. You're not dying, the baby looks healthy, there might be a C-section, but everything will in all probability be fine. You should be grateful.

All I say is, it's a been a very sudden change.

I have a roommate on the other side of the curtain, and she is incensed. She is pregnant with twins. She is obese. She has asthma and is awake all night wheezing and gasping, screaming at the nurses. She might have diabetes. She has four others at home. She is a white single mother. The only reason I came in here, she says to the doctor, was to be induced.

The doctor tells her this is something he cannot do—end the pregnancy a month early because she is tired.

You're treating me like I'm stupid, she says. Well, I'm not stupid; I read things.

He says, you were admitted because you indicated you might harm yourself or the babies.

I didn't say that.

That's what your doctor said.

He was wrong. Maybe his English wasn't good enough.

Well, maybe there was a misunderstanding, the doctor says to her. He retreats, tries to talk about sleep medication. But she is not done with him.

Now, wait, she says, this is quite a misunderstanding, wouldn't you say?

From my side of the room, I hear every word. I don't want to be hearing this, but I do.

She checks out the next day, still pregnant, with medication to help her get a good night's sleep.

I have a new roommate now on the other side of the curtain. A black girl, twelve, maybe thirteen. She is on the phone, mad as a hornet. When is someone going to come to get me? I want to go *now*, she is whining. The doctor said I can go. When do you get off work? She is going down a list of the people she knows who are able to drive: Why can't *he* come and get me, why can't *she* come and get me? Nobody is going to come to get her anytime soon; nobody is swooping in to take her home. She sits on the side of the bed, ready to go, bag set, coat lying on the bed next to her hip. She sits there for two hours watching cartoons.

Already it requires too much effort to explain to the others outside. Where do I start? The pregnancy was going fine. In fact, I was hiking a few weeks ago. Or a joke about a doctor actually waiting? Or get right to the point, right to the definition of preeclampsia. Preeclampsia, I tell them, is the development of hypertension, albuminuria, or edema between the twentieth week of pregnancy and the end of the first week postpartum. In other words, high blood pressure, protein in the urine, or swelling, and I am three for three. My mother-in-law asks, is it what we used to call *toxemia*? So this becomes part of the explanation: It's what they used to call toxemia.

I am on the phone with my mother, trying not to alarm her. I am speaking about the condition abstractly, as something that may or may not have anything to do with me, because the diagnosis is not yet certain. I answer her questions. She is persistent. I may not even have preeclampsia; it might be something else. Then I am saying, preeclampsia can be a precursor to eclampsia, which is very dangerous. As I say this, I become disoriented. Has someone told me this, or did I invent it? My mother presses me for more information. She is relentless. What is eclampsia? I have no idea what I'm talking about; I am talking over my head. I don't even know if I have *pre*eclampsia. I have reached the limits of what I know, I am spent, and, for a second, in my brain, particles are flashing at points outside the circuitry. I need to stop talking, but my mother will not let me hang up. She needs more information.

Preeclampsia. Months later, when the baby is scooting around on his back, I look it up. I want to see it in black and white. Preeclampsia, it says, occurs in five percent of pregnant women, characteristically in women who are pregnant for the first time, primigravidas, and in women with preexisting hypertension and vascular disease. If untreated, it usually smolders for a variable length of time and suddenly progresses to eclampsia, which is often fatal if untreated.

On the contrary, I am being treated. This is why I am in a hospital bed being monitored, poked, pricked, my arm squeezed by an inflated blood pressure cuff. Nurses and doctors push the skin of my ankle with their thumbs to see how far it indents; this is called *pitting*, a way of checking water retention. They knock my shin with a reflex hammer or the sides of their hands to make sure my leg does not spring up too much, because this would be a sign of neurological impairment.

The word *eclampsia* is kept at arm's length from me. No one utters this word without prefix.

Even minor activity makes my blood pressure rise. I have to schedule things, organize my day. Breakfast, shower. Rest. Rest. Read. Rest.

A phone call. Rest. Unexpected visits are not a pleasant surprise. I cannot tolerate them. My responsibility is to not become agitated and to keep an uninterrupted blood flow going through vessels toward the placenta.

A friend comes to visit me in the hospital. She brings a bunch of yellow sweetheart roses. But she brings nothing to put them in. Don't you understand? I cannot even get up to walk down the hall to ask for a paper cup.

I am too high risk now for the nurse-midwives, and one of them comes to visit to ease the transition. She explains to me how high blood pressure puts pressure on the heart and in turn the kidneys, how the kidneys start to slow down, do not discharge enough uric waste, how this leads to swelling. I have already heard it from several doctors and nurses, but she adds her own portentous footnote: The greatest killer of women in childbirth in the Third World is preeclampsia.

Everything about me is now open to comment, even the book I am reading, *The Count of Monte Cristo*. One thousand ninety-five pages. It should see me through. Many episodes. Travel. A robust cast of characters: Edmond Dantès, his love, Mercédès, the mentor, Monsieur Morrel, the plotters, Danglars and Caderousse, the ambitious magistrate, Villefort, set against the backdrop of Napoleonic France.

Shouldn't you be reading something lighter? Every visitor who enters the room asks this.

Actually, I say, it's a page-turner.

Lying on my left side, book in right hand, right arm contorted like a mating swan's neck, wrist bent, I read:

Dantès passed through all the degrees of misfortune that prisoners, forgotten in their dungeon, suffer. He commenced with pride, a natural consequence of hope, and a consciousness of innocence; then he began to doubt his own innocence. . . . Dantès entreated to be removed from his present dungeon into another; for a change, however disadvantageous, was still a change, and could afford him some amusement.

I ask to be moved to a private room, away from wheezing and cartoons, and unlike poor Dantès, I am granted my request.

There is talk again of a cesarean. There may not be enough time for labor. They talk about a rapid-change, life-threatening, worst-case scenario. They will be surprised if I go beyond thirty-four weeks. I definitely will not go full term.

Wait, wait, it's not time. I want to cry and cry and cry, but if I do my blood pressure will rise. It's important to stay as calm as possible. The baby is who matters. And me. If the baby comes now, everything would be fine, but it would be better if it could go longer. I tell myself, I will be fine. The baby will be fine. I need to not let fear grow too big, but this is the first time I have ever thought, I do not want to die. Then, I admonish myself, hysteria does no one any good.

Still, I am terrified by the thought of a premature baby. Premature babies are not in my experience. My nieces and nephews were all born healthy, seven pounds or more. Doctors, nurses, are all telling me that the baby is big enough and will most likely do very well even if he or she were to be born today. This is not a baby in the danger zone. We have babies who are born at twenty-four, twenty-five weeks, one of the consulting doctors says. Now, that's when you worry.

Yes, I think, but the baby may not go home with me; may need to be on a respirator. Yes, but they're so little, so fragile, I won't know how to touch one.

They're not as fragile as you think, a nurse says. I am going to take you down to the intensive-care nursery. You and your husband can see the babies. Then you'll know what to expect. Do you think that would help?

I think that would help, I agree.

I am wheeled past the nursery, past the bank of windows. It is the first time I have seen babies. A surge. This is why I am here. New. Born. Their names written on index cards at the feet of the little plastic bins they lie in. Wrapped in white blankets with blue and pink strips at the tops. Little caps on their heads.

There is a square button to push. An electronic door opens. We are in a washing room, a postpartum mudroom. You put on one of these, the nurse says, and pulls out two hospital gowns from a stack on a shelf, one for my husband, one for me. And then you wash your hands. There is a deep sink behind us. Foot pedals activate the water. In order to reach the faucet, I must stand up. I feel lightheaded, not having sat up this long in days. We scrub up. I sit back down. There is another door to go through, opened by pressing another square button.

The lights are intensely bright. A nursery should be quiet, but there is buzzing and electronic beeping, voices squawking over the intercom. Except for diapers, the babies are all uncovered, naked under heat lamps. The first one I see is a tiny, tiny girl, tiny as a little bird, with delicate limbs and translucent skin, and it is so terrifying, so overwhelming, and I am thinking, Which of these babies is going to survive, which will not? Who will not be well? But even as I am grieving for some of these other infants—which ones I do not know, but statistically for some percentage of them—I am asking the nurse about the weight of one in particular, silently trying to estimate the size of the babies, comparing them to the one inside me: How much does that one weigh? What about this one? What I am doing is profane, and I am ashamed of my relief.

Out of the blue, I am discharged, and I leave with three plastic bracelets on my wrist. At home, my husband gets scissors, cuts them off right away. As soon as they are gone, I am angry. I am not ready to take them off yet. I need them on my wrist, clicking. You have been through something, the bracelets say.

At home, I am required to keep a record of my vital signs, monitor the level of protein in my urine, record any weight gain. I take my blood pressure three times a day, both in a sitting position and lying flat on my back. Blood pressure is more elevated lying flat on my back, the result of thirty extra pounds pressing down upon the vena cava.

If blood pressure is high, I am supposed to lie on my side and see if it will improve. It is high. I lie back down, mumble a series of if-then clauses, bargaining with the cosmos. I lie still, eyes closed. Under the lids, little points of flashing light. I open my eyes; it's unbearable to have them shut.

I stare at the wall in the bedroom. At a hairline crack in the plaster, arabesques on the heat register. I listen to the tinkling of tinfoil that I had put inside the vent, a homemade attempt to regulate air flow.

I arrange objects so I don't have to get up from the living room couch: books, notecards, my *Patient's Record Book*, blood pressure machine, phone, address book, pad of paper. I put everything in arm's reach. It's important to drink a lot of fluid, so there is a pitcher of water and a glass nearby on the end table.

The phone rings. I move my arm behind me slowly, groping. I jostle a book, which hits the cards, which knocks over the glass, which spills the water all over the floor.

At night, my body keeps waking me up. A cough. A sneeze.

In the morning, sitting at the kitchen table, I read in the newspaper that Fellini has died. That they never were able to have a baby. *E la nave va*. And the ship sails.

Adria Bernardi

From the sofa, on my side, I look out at the limbs of the trees. A brilliant cardinal settles in the evergreen, his bilged and tawny mate beside him. If I had known I was going to end up here, I would have washed the windows.

I try to outguess the blood flow, try to pick a time when blood pressure will be low. I take it at different times of the day, trying to outsmart it, but at 8:25 A.M. Saturday morning, it is 153 over 104 in a sitting position, and it does not go down for the second reading. There's no doubt what the doctor is going to say, and he says it: Congratulations, you've earned yourself a trip to the hospital.

Again, the hospital morning ritual. Waking to the sound of the scale being rolled down the hall. Blood pressure, temperature taken. Being checked for signs of swelling. Blood being drawn. Any headache? Nausea? Blurred vision?

I bathe, brush my hair, brush my teeth. Return to bed tired out. Watch TV news. I have grown much too attached to Katie Couric, who is now on vacation, and I am annoyed with her for going, irritated by her replacement.

Midmorning, two disks, transducers, are coated with gel and strapped onto my belly. One monitors the baby's heart, the other uterine contractions. I can locate the baby's heartbeat every time, above my navel, a little to the right. The baby moves, squirms away from the transducer. Smart baby.

They give me a metal cylinder with a button at the top that I am to press with my thumb whenever the baby moves. I'll be hooked up for one half-hour, longer if the baby does not move enough. They are looking for *acceleration*, the baby's heart beating faster when he or she moves. I cannot read or talk on the phone. I must concentrate on waiting for a kick, trying to discern if it is a kick or a hiccup, which does not count as movement. Lying on my side, facing the machine, I try to read the printout as it snakes and loops over itself in midair. I fall asleep to the sound of the baby's heartbeat. We take a little nap together.

My lab values improve, worsen, improve, worsen. This is an unusual presentation, my doctor says. Generally lab values do not improve. The only cure for preeclampsia, he says, is labor and delivery. He asks me how *The Count of Monte Cristo* is progressing.

You know what it's about, don't you?

No, he says.

Well, I say, it's about someone who is unjustly imprisoned and languishes in a cell for years and after he gets out, he spends the rest of his life seeking revenge.

The doctor staggers back in mock horror. Oh, no! And he clutches his heart.

I keep reminding myself that I am here for something joyful. At every turn, the doctors have said the baby looks good. The end of this illness will bring, if all goes well—and there is no reason to believe differently—a child. Even so, I am eroding. Visitors tiptoe around me, afraid to sit down, afraid to wear me out, commenting on the flowers. Oh, these peach-colored roses are stupendous, I've never seen a rose so huge. It's true, they are stupendous, and so are the mauve roses, and the basket of cut flowers with baby's breath; they are all stupendous. Even as I am agreeing with them, appreciating the concern, I resent having this conversation about flowers, nearly in tears because I am so diminished that I am desperate to converse about flowers and who they came from and how wonderful they smell.

Tap, tap. The nurse searches for a good spot on my hand. It's like a needle shot, she says. A prick.

You are going to put a thing inside me that is going to stay there?

And now there is a catheter in the top of my right hand. A Hep-Lock. It is a small metal plate with teeth, a piece of hardware, like something from the bracket aisle, a corner bracket with teeth. There is a clear, curved plastic tube attached. It is a violation, a first-time perforation of my skin, an opening to the possible inevitability of a future with more catheters—that is to say, not a time of youth but of moving in the other direction. I am not supposed to be thinking about these things, about mortality, things that will make me grieve, send my blood pressure up.

In the grand scheme of things the insertion of a Hep-Lock is a toe-stub; it's a nothing procedure. But there is a tube in my vein, the on-ramp to my heart. To get medication there. An anticonvulsant. Just in case. They have made me IV accessible.

Held in a Hep-Lock. Helpless. Not hip, not hep. A Hep-Lock grip. *Heparin*, an anticoagulant, a blood thinner used to flush out the catheter and keep it clean. From *hepar*, Greek for *liver*. *Hep*, a variant of *hip*, the fruit of a rose-tree. *Hep*, an obscure form of *heap*, which is where I find myself, locked on my side, all the weight of my body concentrated in the bone of my hip, lying in a primigravida heap.

In the middle of the night, I wake to click-click as a thermometer is inserted into a portable machine, then extracted, sheathed in a plastic tube and slid underneath my tongue. The blood pressure cuff inflates around my upper arm, then hisses as it exhales. It is a drifting time, broken by digital beeps.

Then it is six A.M. and still dark. I'm washing my face. I look at myself in the mirror, at my eyes, which are lost in my bloated face, and from out of nowhere come the words to a song I barely know, *Low, low, low.* I walk back to the bed slowly. My belly pushes the hospital gown to its limit. My naked ankles and calves are way down below. My swollen feet press against my slippers.

I am back in bed, teeth and hair brushed. Before I can shower, I have to wait for a nurse who will wrap a plastic bag around my hand to protect the Hep-Lock. A man comes in to collect the hazardous waste, the needles and syringes from a box on the wall behind the bed that says, *Basura Infeccioso.*

I cross yesterday off my calendar. I do not cross a day off until I wake up the next day.

A medical technician comes in to draw blood. He takes my right arm, taps it hard, high and low. Drops it, exasperated. Takes my left arm, taps it hard. Grunts. All the good spots are taken.

The room is dirty from the day before, newspapers and Styrofoam cups overflowing in the wastebasket. A food tray not taken away. On the floor, between bed and bathroom, drops of blood have splattered, dripped from the Hep-Lock, which has come loose. I begin to fear infection. I start asking, How long can this thing stay in my hand before it has to be changed? My hand aches. When you pay this much attention to your body, something is bound to start hurting.

The people coming in look so good; they are all wearing winter gloves. My husband looks handsome, dashing: neat hair, nice tie, his wedding band, a watch on his wrist, his smart wool overcoat, the belt looped behind. I am the cardinal's bilge-water mate.

The Count has begun to wind down in the last two hundred pages. Caderousse, the plotter, is dead, and the intrigue starts to be revealed to each of the characters.

The baby looks great, the doctor says, is moving well; the breathing movements are good.

Before, I wanted a daughter. Now, lying flat on my back, gel smeared all over my belly, a transducer being passed over my skin as the doctor interprets movement on the black-and-white screen, measuring head size, femur, stomach, I think, whoever you are, you are the baby I want.

The book is over. Now what?

In the morning, my reflexes are brisker, hands more swollen, blood pressure higher. I was awake between midnight and six.

The doctor says, it's time.

The baby is coming now, no more waiting. I should feel excited. Instead, I am filled with an overwhelming sense of failure. The baby was entitled to the full time inside, and I could not provide it.

They put me on a gurney, not into a wheelchair. That night a prostaglandin gel is spread over my cervix to start the dilation process. A blood pressure cuff remains on my arm twenty-four hours, automatically inflating and deflating, recording at regular intervals. I face the IV pole, the contraction monitors, the bathroom. Certain nurses leave lights off, turn them on when necessary, apologize. Others flip the lights on, talk loudly, make noise. Their night is day; why should they tiptoe around?

The second day, Tuesday, there is hardly any change at all, and prostaglandin gel is applied again. The third day, Wednesday, I am barely dilated, but enough to insert a laminaria, a thin stick made from seaweed. Incredible pain when it is inserted, pressing against me, and I fear for the baby, that it will be too much trauma. Twelve hours later, they are able to insert two more. I call them *joss sticks*, you know, incense sticks, but no one laughs at my joke.

My back is to the window. This is another one of my jokes: Now that I finally have a room with a view outside, I have to lie with my back to it.

I search for the right expression for this irony, a figure of speech. *Putting icing on the cake. Adding injury to insult.* Words exit my mouth, only approximately correct, out of sequence. There is a hairline disjunction between what I am articulating and what I want to articulate. After I say it, I am rethinking, reformulating. Is this a glimmer of what it is to have a stroke?

Down the hall, piercing screams in the middle of the night. Then an infant crying. When the nurse comes in, I ask if everyone is all right.

Yes, a beautiful baby boy.

Wonderful, I say.

I hate births like this, she says.

Why?

They're fine for a few hours, and then it's horrible. The tremors start, the constant crying, another one addicted to cocaine.

My husband brings in a radio. I have him set it behind me, and it leans against my back.

Later we have a fight. He has taken the remote control. I had put it just above my head, above the pillow, balanced just so. A precarious placement, granted, but I could reach it. Now I can't find it, and he is not in the room. When he returns, a fight erupts weakly, distilled. Over the remote control. This is what it has come to.

I am bigger, bigger, I have the sensation that my eyes are on my cheeks. There is no point trying to nicen-up. I haven't bathed for days and am sweet, sticky from sponge baths.

The nurse is washing my body. I am grateful for the human contact, someone washing my hands, my feet; warm, soapy water, warm rinse, clean, dry towel. I am embarrassed that I crave physical contact so much that a bath at the hands of a stranger in a room lit with fluorescent light, with the click of the IV drips, and an overhead pager saying, Doctor So-and-So, please call the operator, is so welcome. It has taken no time at all to break me down into a patient.

The contractions begin hard, induced by Pitocin, which is dripping into me. The pain is a deep knot, in waves, a cramping. The nurse offers no encouragement or suggestions. I am alone; my husband has taken one of his few breaks. Exhale on the pain? Inhale on it? I can't remember. I am mixed up, uncoordinated, as if I'm trying to pat my head and make a circle on my stomach at the same time.

Diligent, I search for an image to take my mind off the pain. I try visualizing a flower. Then I remember reading, Whatever you do, do *not* visualize a flower at the beginning of labor, only at the end of labor, when pushing, and I am nowhere near the end of labor. But there it is, a yellow dahlia. It begins to pulsate. Bigger, smaller. Bigger, smaller.

I try another image: a tidal pool at the end of a barrier island. I walk toward it, along the beach, water gently lapping. I circle the tidal pool, tannin-brown and full of tiny fish. I trace the shape of the pool with my eyes, and this takes me away from the pain until the gentle lapping turns into cresting and crashing.

I start again. It is a long walk to the tip of the island. Pace yourself. You don't want to get there too soon because then the walk will be over, and you'll have to find another image, and while you're searching for a new image, the contractions will overtake you.

The doctor is here, and he explains the options: Stadol or an epidural. Once I get an epidural I won't be able to get up again. Stadol is effective only for a limited period of time. I am trying to concentrate, but it is as if I am falling asleep and missing whole segments of the conversation. It seems, on one hand, Stadol will be less intrusive, less drastic than the epidural, which means a needle stuck into the back, which, if they miss, means paralysis. These are the things going through my mind. I am thinking of my vertebrae, my marrow. The pain starts again while I try to ask questions. Twinge. Cramp. Surge. It prompts swift decision. Stadol it is.

Instantaneously, the pain is smothered, cut off from me. I am drowsy and loose, saying to my husband, I can see why people use heroin. I am dreamy and relaxed but also exhilarated. There is a distant, muffled throbbing; not pain, just a slight, regularly recurring, rounded bumping along the edge of my belly, far away on the other side of the globe, in the middle of the Pacific Ocean. Oh, it is a pleasant sensation. I think the stick men are coming, and by this I mean a stick figure that will become the visual image of whatever I am saying, so that if I say, *And then he walked upstairs . . .* , a stick figure will appear, legs bent at the knees, climbing up a stick staircase. I am in labor with my own private cartoon. I would like to watch my words illustrate themselves for a while. It would be such a diversion. The throb is far off, a dollop, a little drop on the Doppler scale. I can crack a joke or two, step outside my body again, but when I tell my husband about the stick man, which is very amusing to me, comforting even, I sense he thinks I am incoherent.

I am awakened by an enormous knife-boom, a punch at the edge of my belly. The medication has worn off. I opt for the Stadol again because I still believe it would be worse to have a needle stuck into my back. I expect the second infusion to be effective as immediately and as completely as the first one, but it is not. The spasm is dulled, the edge is not as sharp, but the pain is just as deep. My body is already addicted to the Stadol; it takes a big dose for the same effect, and the pain can already outwit it.

What time of day is it? Laboriously, I think it through. I roll onto my back and turn my head to look out the window. It's dark. It must be the middle of Wednesday night.

Adria Bernardi

I wake up with what is inside my body hurling itself against a wall trying to get out, and suddenly the expression, *to jump out of one's skin* makes sense. I am afraid. Afraid of what? How will the story end? Every thought turns ugly. The yellow dahlia keeps blossoming again and again, close to my face, in hyper-color. It will not stop throbbing. It hurts my eyes, terrifies me.

To calm myself I imagine a hiking trail, dense with rhododendron, mountain laurel, ferns. I'm walking along it, fine, fine, until the trail makes an abrupt turn to the left and I am teetering above a gorge.

I call out to my husband. *What is wrong with me that I cannot calm myself? Every thought turns to disaster.*

Stadol can make you fretful, he says. This reassures me, knowing that my fears are drug-induced.

I sleep fitfully, then wake thinking of my great-grandmother. I tell myself that I cannot allow myself to think of Cherubina, sweet-faced, dead four days after childbirth. Were there signs, was it sudden, no hemorrhaging? A stroke, which swiftly, unexpectedly, killed her? No, I tell myself, now is not the time to think of her. Instead, I think of my great-grandmothers Angelina and Carolina, and then they are there, gripping me with callused hands. Strength, strength, they say, you will emerge on the other side of this. This is no time to be weak. It is not a visitation, they are not ghosts, but my wrists are surely bruised.

In the morning, they stand me up to be weighed. I am woozy. My water breaks, very warm over my legs. It spills all over the scale and flows onto the floor. I apologize. I am so sorry someone will have to clean it up. But there is also relief, a flash of excitement that there is progress in this labor after two days of prostaglandin and joss sticks. After days of complying and complying, pliant, plaintive on my side, and my body not doing its part.

I am sitting on the side of the bed, leaning over, my back exposed. The doctor puts the needle in just to the right of my lower spine. Then she moves a pin up and down my leg, trunk, upper body. Can you feel this? This? This? Evaluating the epidural.

I am lying on my side. I put my hand on a pillow. I thought my pillow was under my head. Then I realize my hand is resting on my thigh. My leg feels nothing. My hand tells my brain that my leg is a pillow.

Then they're ready to start the magnesium sulfate. The Mag. The nurses hang plastic bags on the hooks at the top of the IV pole. They hang them up offhandedly, like shirts ready to be picked up at the dry cleaners. The first bag is called the bolus. The liquid entering hurts, a little ache on the top of the hand. As it empties into my body, I can trace its course. There is a tingling sensation, a warmth. Then the warmth becomes unpleasant, though not painful. There is a pulse of heat in my gums, above my teeth. My whole body is hot, then burning. A surge comes from the back of my skull, arcs forward to my cheeks, like a sheet pulled over the top of my head and dropped in front of my eyes. It is a blur. It happens very fast, this progression from heat to blur. The light hurts when I open my eyes. Stars swirl and make me dizzy, a blizzard that is white and throbbing.

I have a towel over my head, a wet cloth that my husband keeps replacing. It dries and warms as soon as it touches my forehead. I am demanding, impatient, imploring. Change it. I need a cold cloth.

I need my eyes covered. I do not see anything during the final stages of labor, the doctor, the nurse, my husband. To take the cloth off my head makes me dizzy, nauseated. My head is way too big around the cranium. Take a tape measure, check and see if it isn't abnormally big. It is dark and quiet, I am not saying much, groaning, moaning; my head is against my husband's shoulder, leaning against him. I am sitting up. He is supporting me, telling me what he sees, what is happening, that I am doing well.

The pediatrician has just come in. My husband whispers to me, very quietly, hushed, like an announcer at a golf tournament: They're getting the baby's things ready now. The incubator. We're that close.

Somehow I decide I will not scream. It has nothing to do with dignity. I have calculated the amount of energy required for a scream. I can expend nothing except to push the baby out. Round and stretching, the pain, pushing, squeezing, like you are having a bowel movement, the doctor says. Push from the back, not the front, I am thinking, I do not want to rip.

The baby's head, I can see the baby's head, the doctor says. Do you want to touch it? No, I am so afraid, afraid of the soft spot, afraid I will hurt it, afraid to stop concentrating, afraid to hex it.

A round of pushing. In between, I lie back down. Then sit back up. I need to take in a deep breath over the count of ten, let it go out to the count of a slow ten. The pain occurs while breathing out. Numbers help, something else for the brain to register besides pain. My eyes closed, I see each number in order, between eyeball and lid, bold and colorful, like a letter on a child's wooden block.

He is wet and glistening, and his face is full of anguish, red-faced outrage. A little, tiny manlike face. Legs bent at knees and pulled up.

Come here, let me hold you.

The next twenty-four hours, I cannot drink enough. Except for ice cubes, I have had nothing to eat or drink for four days. I keep ringing the nurses' buzzer. More juice. More water. As soon as they bring me one glass, it is empty and I call for another one.

I cannot get up to go and see my son. I am still on my side, still hooked up to the magnesium sulfate. He is so far away, alone, under bright white lights with an IV in his tiny hand, his heels covered with round Band-Aids where they have stuck him again and again to make sure his glucose level is staying up. A baby who is in the intensive-care unit, hearing bells and beeps, having tiny tremors, a sign of prematurity, and I cannot get there to him, cannot even will myself to demand to be taken there; I am unable to move. This is his entry into the world, not cuddled, cradled, but lying there in a plastic box under white lights.

The magnesium sulfate has dripped into me for six days. It has been pumped in, one to two grams per hour, given to diminish the risk of convulsion or worse. I am in a darkened room, cannot stand to have the lights turned on. I say to anyone who comes near me, to nurses and doctors, to family members, my husband, the person who draws my blood—only the person delivering flowers is spared—I say to anyone who comes into my room, say it out of context, say it often, This magnesium sulfate is wicked, get it out of me.

It is the second day after the birth, and I am still complaining. The baby is here. He is fine. I am fine. I cannot tolerate it anymore, the exhaustion, the being awakened for vital signs. My vision is blurred, my eyes ache and sting, my face is flushed and burning. My mouth is sand. I have been in the dark for six days with this liquid dripping inside of me, click, click. It is wicked, wicked stuff, I say to the doctor. Stop it, can't you stop it?

He tells me it has to stay in for a while longer.

I can't believe it; I can't take it anymore. He asks me if I knew there was an incident with a patient with preeclampsia the other night. No, I say matter-of-factly, displaying my grasp of reality. Did someone have a seizure?

No, he says. She had a stroke.

Silence. Pause. Okay. Well, leave the Hep-Lock in me then.

In the middle of the night, I walk down the corridor, dragging the IV pole along with me. On the right at the end of the hall, there is a room. The door is open. The lights are on. A woman lies flat in a hospital bed. Her straight dark hair is pulled away from her face. She is a mirror of me. She is sleeping, her face is so smooth—too smooth. She is hooked up to a ventilator.

I drag myself back through the hall, sore and bruised, into my room and clamber up again into the hospital bed. Who is she, poor woman? I grab my wrist to calm myself, fingers encircling the bone. I have not had a seizure. I have not had a stroke. My baby boy is fine; he is tiny, but he will be fine. I have been given a glimpse of certain eventualities. I must tolerate the wicked mag. It is not so bad, I think, as I lie in the dark, eyes open, seeing stars.

Adria Bernardi is this year's winner of the Editors' Prize in Essay. She is widely published as an essayist, fiction writer and translator.

Ernest J. Gaines

© Jerry Bauer

Ernest J. Gaines is the author of six novels, including *Of Love and Dust*, *The Autobiography of Miss Jane Pittman* and *A Gathering of Old Men*, and one collection of stories, *Bloodline*. His most recent novel, *A Lesson Before Dying*, won the National Book Critics Circle Award in 1993. He has received a literary award from the American Academy of Arts and Letters, a Guggenheim Fellowship and a MacArthur Foundation Fellowship. Gaines was born on a plantation near New Roads, Louisiana. He now divides his time between Lafayette, Louisiana, and San Francisco. This interview was conducted by Jennifer Levasseur and Kevin Rabalais on the University of Southwestern Louisiana campus in Lafayette on August 26, 1998.

An Interview with Ernest J. Gaines/ *Jennifer Levasseur and Kevin Rabalais*

Interviewer: You've been writer-in-residence at the University of Southwestern Louisiana since 1984. What do you feel are your responsibilities as a teacher of creative writing?

Gaines: I approach the teaching of creative writing—if you can possibly teach creative writing—from the Socratic method. The students have their material ready on Tuesdays, and they will have read and written critiques of the material by the next time we meet. I write a critique as well. Each Tuesday night, we discuss two students' work. The students who have stories being discussed that night read aloud for five or ten minutes so we can feel the rhythm. After the student reads, I open it up for discussion. I don't lecture. I sit back and direct the discussion; if it slows down, I speed it up, or if no one has anything to say, I raise a question. This is my approach to "teaching" writing. I set requirements. I believe the students should all write critiques of each other's work, and they must also discuss the stories in class. I feel students usually learn as much about writing from discussion among their peers as they do from me. I don't assign books for them to read because they should read everything. I always recommend books— the Bible, Strunk and White's *The Elements of Style*. My six words of advice to writers are: "Read, read, read, write, write, write." Writing is a lonely job; you have to read, and then you must sit down at the desk and write. There's no one there to tell you when to write, what to write, or how to write. I tell students if they are going to be writers, they must sit down at a desk and write every day.

Interviewer: The students read from their own work for the first few minutes of class so readers can get the sound of the rhythm. You've also said you write your stories to be read aloud.

Gaines: When people hear stories, they identify more closely with the characters. When I read aloud, people always come up to me and say, "I understand it much better now that I've heard you read it. I can hear the characters' voices much clearer." Many of the students use dialects or words and phrases we are not familiar with, but once we hear it, we tend to understand it much better.

Interviewer: Dialogue is something you've said you are proud of in your work.

Gaines: In dialogue, I'm dealing with the sounds I've heard. One of the reasons I often write from first person or multiple points of view is to hear the voices of different characters. Omniscient narration becomes a problem because, for me, the omniscient is my own voice narrating the story and then bringing in characters for dialogue.

Interviewer: There is a strength in the many voices in your work, a weight you give to each character's voice no matter how small a role he or she plays. One very minor character, a drunk in *In My Father's House,* gives Reverend Martin directions. When he speaks, his voice is as strong as any in the novel.

Gaines: My ear is pretty good. As a small child, I listened to radio a lot. During that time—this was back in the late '40s—there were always great dramas and actors on radio. I liked listening to them because I had to follow the story through dialogue. I like reading plays, and I like listening to the ways people speak.

Interviewer: Does this oral approach help when you are editing your work?

Gaines: What I usually do is record my work on a tape recorder. If it sounds good, then it is. I never read my work to anyone else and say, "Okay, what do you think?" Editors recommend certain things, but usually, at this point in the game, I can stick to my guns and say, "This is how it's written, and this is how it sounds." I write about south Louisiana, and I feel my ear is pretty good for the dialects of that region, at least better than the people in New York who have never been here.

"You learn from music, from watching great athletes at work—how disciplined they are, how they move."

Interviewer: In *The Autobiography of Miss Jane Pittman*, it is Miss Jane the reader sees and hears. How did you find Miss Jane's voice?

Gaines: I did a lot of research to get the historical facts right and read quite a few slave narratives to see how the slaves expressed themselves and how they used their vocabularies. I grew up on a plantation on False River, Louisiana, and I was around older people—my aunt, who raised me, and the older people who visited her because she was crippled and couldn't walk. Those were the voices I had in mind while creating Miss Jane Pittman. She was not based on any one person or any two people but on the kind of experience someone who lived during that time might have gone through. Her voice came fairly easily. I had read enough, and could recall the dialects and the limited vocabularies of the older people on the plantation where I lived, to create an authentic voice for Miss Jane. The first draft was told from multiple points of view, with people talking about her after she had died. I did that for more than a year and then realized it was not exactly right. I needed to get her to tell the story, so I concentrated on one voice rather than several.

Interviewer: Have there been some characters' voices that were easier to get into than others?

Gaines: Jim's in *Of Love and Dust* because I was thirty-three years old when I started writing that book, and I created him to be the same age. He's uneducated, but he's thirty-three years old. He uses the language I grew up around living in Louisiana. Also, it wasn't too difficult to find Jefferson's diary voice in *A Lesson Before Dying* because I wrote the diary after working on the novel for five years. I knew his character and what he would say, how he would express himself. Sometimes I have to rewrite and rewrite to get the exact phrases I want. I stick with south Louisiana, not places with unfamiliar accents.

"When people hear stories, they identify more closely with the characters."

Interviewer: How do you approach a novel like *A Gathering of Old Men*, with its distinct multiple points of view?

Gaines: I try to concentrate on voices of different people I knew as a child. I left Louisiana at fifteen but always came back. While writing *A Gathering of Old Men*, I could recall that different people spoke differently and they would never describe the same thing the same way; they never used the same expressions. So when I went from one of the characters in that novel to another, I had to concentrate entirely on that character and how he would express himself. Then when I went to another character, I would concentrate on another person's voice and give it to that particular character.

Interviewer: You've said before that you were influenced by Japanese films, including *Rashomon*, the story of a murder told from several points of view.

Gaines: I saw *Rashomon* many years ago, and it has had some effect on me, as have Faulkner, Joyce and whoever else's work I've read. They say if you steal from one person you are plagiarizing, but if you steal from a hundred people you are a genius. You don't pick entirely from Faulkner, entirely from *Rashomon*, or entirely from Hemingway. You learn from all of them, just as all writers have done. You learn from people you read.

Interviewer: What are some other important influences on your work?

Gaines: I've been influenced by the great French filmmakers of the '50s—Truffaut, for example, particularly *The 400 Blows* and *Shoot the Piano Player*. When I was writing *A Lesson Before Dying*, I saw a film on television with Danny Glover, and it had a tremendous effect on me.

Danny Glover plays a social worker who visits prisons. There is one prisoner who will do anything to annoy him. The little things he would do to irritate Danny Glover made me think, "Hey, that's good!" I've never been to visit anybody in prison repeatedly. A couple of weeks ago, I was talking with some kids in a jail in Orlando, Florida. These were murderers, dope peddlers. They were sixteen and seventeen years old. But I've never gone back and forth like Grant does in *A Lesson Before Dying*. Watching this film with Danny Glover, I thought, "This is what happens when you keep going back to a prison to visit one guy. He will always do something to irritate you." That's how I decided to have Jefferson not speak, or say something to annoy Grant. What I'm saying is that you learn from all these things. You learn from music, from watching great athletes at work—how disciplined they are, how they move. You learn these things by watching a shortstop at work, how he concentrates on one thing at a time. You learn from classic music, from the blues and jazz, from bluegrass. From all this, you learn how to sustain a great line without bringing in unnecessary words. I advise my students to keep their antennae out so they can pick things up from all these sources, everything life has to offer, but books especially, which is the main tool they have to work with. They should not close their ears or eyes to anything that surrounds them.

Interviewer: One book you've recommended is *Max Perkins: Editor of Genius* by A. Scott Berg. How do you feel about the hands-on style of editing, exemplified by Perkins, that doesn't seem to be as present in the publishing world today?

Gaines: I really like Maxwell Perkins because of all the great writers who were around him. A. Scott Berg did a wonderful job with that book. He did a lot of research and brought out the different characters of F. Scott Fitzgerald, Ernest Hemingway and Thomas Wolfe. I knew some good critics and editors. Malcolm Cowley, who had the sense to rediscover Faulkner, was a teacher of mine at Stanford. Wallace Stegner was my mentor at Stanford. He was the person who brought me there. Ed (E.L.) Doctorow, who later became famous as a writer himself, was my editor at Dial Press. He was a very good editor. I have a good editor at Knopf now, Ash Green. These people are wonderful. They are not as famous as Max Perkins, and not all writers are fortunate enough to get great editors, but I've been lucky. You need a good editor because every writer thinks he can write a *War and Peace*, but by the time he gets it on paper, it's not *War and Peace* anymore; it's comic-book stuff. If you have an honest editor who knows what literature and writing are about, he can give you good advice. You don't necessarily have to follow it all. It's good to get the material away from you after you've finished something, to send it out and let another person comment on it. I had a wonderful agent, Dorothea Oppenheimer, and she saw everything of mine for thirty-one years. We had our fights. When she criticized me, I would say, "Well, you don't know what you're talking about. I'm the writer." But I apologized later. I think those editors and agents are necessary. I didn't get along with all my editors, though.

Interviewer: You began work on what later became your first novel, *Catherine Carmier*, when you were sixteen years old. It went through many rewrites and titles. What type of learning process was this?

Gaines: I tried to write a novel around 1949, which later became *Catherine Carmier*. Of course, I sent it to New York, to a publisher, and they sent it back. We had an incinerator in the back yard, and I burned it. I was falling back in my class work, so I started concentrating on school. When I was twenty, I went into the army. I wrote a little bit. I came out when I was twenty-two and I went to San Francisco State to study literature and theater writing. Then I went to Stanford. I was writing short stories during that time. Someone gave a lecture, and he told us that young writers without a name would have a hard time publishing a collection of stories. So that day, I put the short stories aside and said, "No more short stories. I've got to write something I can publish." I didn't have anything else for a novel but that one story I'd tried to write about ten years earlier. I started rewriting it, and I wrote about fifty pages and won the Joseph Henry Jackson Award, which was a local award given to residents of California. That helped me get through 1959. I got jobs at the post office, a print shop, a bank. I would write in the morning and get these little part-time jobs in the afternoon. From '59 to '64, I wrote that novel over and over. I must have written it more than ten times. Each time I rewrote it, I came up with a different title. I was always changing things: somebody would die in one draft, and another person would die in the next. Malcolm Cowley and several other editors saw it, but no one was ready to publish it. It is a simple story about a guy coming back to the old place and visiting the old people, and he has changed so much that he doesn't fit in anymore. The model I used was Turgenev's *Fathers and Sons*. I was reading something from it every day. It's about a young doctor who has just finished university and comes back to the old place and falls in love with a beautiful woman. He loses her and dies. My character does

"That's what writing should be about: presenting as many facets as you possibly can."

---

the same thing, but he doesn't die. He has to go away again. I was using Turgenev's novel as a model for how to write a novel.

Interviewer: In that novel, you explore a situation—a young man who leaves Louisiana to receive an education, then returns—that you examine again in your most recent novel, *A Lesson Before Dying*.

Gaines: My characters seem like they can't get away. Miss Jane tries to walk to Ohio, but she never gets out of Louisiana. Charlie, in *A Gathering of Old Men*, tries to run away, but he has to come back. All my characters are like that; they go so far, and then they return. They must face up to their responsibilities.

Interviewer: They know they must accept responsibility and go on because it is the graceful thing to do.

Gaines: Yes. They have to make the effort to go on, and sometimes it brings death. But they must make that effort before the moment of death. In *A Lesson Before Dying*, Jefferson must stand before he will be executed. Marcus, in *Of Love and Dust*, can't escape, but he rises before he dies and becomes a better human being. In *A Gathering of Old Men*, Charlie must come back, and he dies when he does. There are certain lines they have to cross to prove their humanity. I could not write about a character who did not have these qualities—a person who struggles and falls but gets up, who will go to a certain point, even though he knows he might get killed. That's a common theme in all my work: those who cannot escape by running away, and those who go to a certain point, even if it means death. For example, in *A Lesson Before Dying*, Grant will not try to run away anymore. Vivian is going to keep him in Louisiana.

"I recommend taking the easiest route in writing, not making things harder than they really are."

Interviewer: In *A Gathering of Old Men,* you give the reader both points of view—black and white—to show what each side is going through and how they are living.

Gaines: That's what writing should be about: presenting as many facets as you possibly can. I'm not interested in seeing one side of anything. One of the reasons I make both Grant and Jefferson tragic figures in *A Lesson Before Dying* is because I wanted this to be a story about more than just a young black man sitting on death row. I needed someone to go to the prison and teach Jefferson, but also someone who would learn while teaching because he is also in a prison; Grant is in a prison of being unable to live the way he would like to live. I had to discover how he could break out of that. Jefferson, of course, finds release in death, and Grant must take on the responsibility of becoming a better person, a better teacher. I did not want a simple story about someone being executed; we have had lots of them, too many. I wanted something else, another added component to that novel.

Interviewer: In your body of work there are examples of almost every point of view.

Gaines: I change point of view when one does not work for me. *A Gathering of Old Men* was originally told from one point of view, that of the newspaperman, Lou Dimes. Then I realized he could not tell the story. He could not see Snookum running and striking his butt the way you would if you were trying to make a horse run faster. He could not see Janie going to that house, and so many other small things that could make the story better. He never would have known the thoughts of these people. So much of the story is internal. There is very little action. You don't see Beau being shot. What you see is Beau lying there and all these other people talking and thinking. I knew I had to write it

---

from multiple points of view rather than omniscient. *The Autobiography of Miss Jane Pittman*, as I have said, began as a multiple-point-of-view narrative, but it did not work. I rewrote it as a first-person narrative. I recommend taking the easiest route in writing, not making things harder than they really are. If you can tell a story better from the omniscient point of view, then tell it that way. If you can tell it better from first person, tell it that way. I never say, "Well, I'm going to tell some first-person stories and some omniscient ones." I think, "What's the easiest way to tell my story without cheating?" I cannot cheat myself in writing.

Interviewer: Earlier, you mentioned that you were warned off trying to publish short-story collections when you began writing. The same warning is given to young writers today.

Gaines: Thirty-five hundred copies of *Catherine Carmier* were printed. Only about 2,500 were sold. The rest were remaindered. I had written the short stories that later appeared in *Bloodline* by the time I wrote *Catherine Carmier*. There are only five, so I may have been writing the fourth. I then wrote another one, the title story, which is the last in that collection. I sent it to Bill Decker at Dial Press, and I said, "Those stories are good; they will make my name." Bill said, "Yes, we know the stories are good, but you need to be a name in order for us to publish them." It's a catch-22. They might make your name, but you need a name before you can publish them. Who's going to pay attention to an unknown young writer? It was then that I wrote *Of Love and Dust*. I wrote the first draft in three months and sent it to Bill Decker. He said, "I like the first part of your novel, and I like the second part, but they don't have anything in common. You need to make it either a farce or a tragedy." I rewrote it in three months and sent it back to him. He said, "You've improved it ninety percent. Now I want you to run it through the typewriter one more time and do anything you want to do because I think you know where you want to go with the novel." I did that and sent it back to him within two months. He told me, "I'll publish it, then I will publish your stories." The novel was published in '64, and the stories were published in the spring of '68. That's how I got my stories published.

Interviewer: You have not published a story collection since *Bloodline*. Have you written stories since then?

Gaines: I've thought about it, but I never came up with any that were in the same class as those. Also, whenever I finished one novel, I was always ready to start another one. I don't have one in mind now, but in the past I've always had a novel in mind while working on another one.

Interviewer: The first story in *Bloodline,* "A Long Day in November," was later revised and published as a children's book with the same title.

Gaines: Yes, we cut out some sexual terms and then added illustrations to make it a children's book. But it's not a children's book. My wife tells me it's still an adult book told by a six-year-old child.

Interviewer: Whose idea was it to turn that story into a children's book?

Gaines: The people at Dial Press recognized that I had two stories in *Bloodline* narrated by children, so they said, "Can you write a children's story?" I said, "I can write a story from a child's point of view, but I don't know anything about writing children's books." Someone at Dial said, "Well, maybe we can take one of these stories." I wish they had taken "The Sky Is Gray." It would have made a much better children's book than "A Long Day in November."

Interviewer: Was writing something you always thought you would do?

Gaines: I did not know I wanted to be a writer as a child in Louisiana. It wasn't until I went to California and ended up in the library and began reading a lot that I knew I wanted to be a writer. I read many great novels and stories and did not see myself or my people in any of them. It was then that I tried to write. There were very few people on the plantation who had any education at all, especially the old people my aunt's age and my grandmother's age. They had never gone to school, and they didn't have any books. I used to write letters for them. I had to listen very carefully to what they had to say and how they said it. I put their stories down on paper, and they would give me teacakes. If I wanted to play ball or shoot marbles, I had to finish writing fast. So I began to create. I wrote about their gardens, the weather, cooking, preserving, anything. I've been asked many times when I started writing. I used to say it was in the small Andrew Carnegie Library in Vallejo, California, but I realize now that it was on the plantation.

"I feel after writing so many pages, maybe at most four hundred, there is nothing else to say so it is time to close it down."

Interviewer: What impact have your many years of teaching had on your writing and reading?

Gaines: My students keep me aware of things around me, but I don't know that my "style"— and I hate using words like that—has changed in any way, or that my views on life have changed in any way from teaching. I do learn things from certain students. Most of my students are middle-class white females. I learn about their ways of thinking and describing things, their backgrounds and social lives. So when I come to write something of my own, that knowledge is there to use, if necessary. For example, when I was writing *A Gathering of Old Men*, I had someone in mind just like Candy. In fact, she's still on that plantation, and she knows I was writing about her in some ways. I am always getting information from the things and people around me, the sounds, the sights, the weather. I do learn from my students, but I don't know how they have changed my view of writing.

Interviewer: In the past, you've said if you had a student come to you who had the potential and desire to create a great work, you would put the student's work in front of your own. Do you feel being a mentor would be as fulfilling as working on your own writing?

Gaines: I can't say that, but I would say the objective of teaching is passing on what you know. I am slowing down now as a writer. Most American writers slow down in their fifties, though some people say I wrote my best book, *A Lesson Before Dying*, at sixty. But I'm not as aggressive now. I'm not writing for five or six hours a day anymore. It's possible to devote more time to a student, to a young writer, and not feel cheated at all. I think I was given a talent to be a writer, and I should use that talent. I don't know that the student's work would be more important than mine—that I would be able to quit writing and

"I've always thought the idea of having things in a single setting and limited to twenty-four hours was the ideal way of telling stories."

---

devote all my time to him or her—but I would give a heck of a lot of time to that work.

Interviewer: Were there goals you set at the beginning of your career?

Gaines: Well, I thought I would win the Nobel Prize. I thought I would make a lot of money and be able to send it back to my aunt who raised me, but she died many years before any of my work had been published. I told myself I would write for five, six hours a day every day and try to have enough money to support myself to write. I wanted to have enough money to write as much as I wanted to write, but I never set any goals to be rich or travel the world.

Interviewer: Your novels are all close in length, but *The Autobiography of Miss Jane Pittman* spans more than one hundred years, while *A Gathering of Old Men* follows characters through one day.

Gaines: I am proud to have accomplished this, to have concentrated on one day with flashbacks, and also to have written something as broad as *The Autobiography of Miss Jane Pittman*. The novels are all about the same number of pages, and the time span in most of them is the same. In *A Lesson Before Dying*, I had to stretch the time to what would be equivalent to the semester of school blacks were getting in the rural South; at that time, we were getting less than six months. I knew exactly the kind of time I had to put into that novel as far as story line, when it would begin and when it would end. But the other novels are all about the same size. I never decided beforehand how long a book would be. It just so happens I learned more from Turgenev than I thought I did in the beginning. His novels were very short compared to Dostoyevsky's or Tolstoy's. I feel after writing so many pages, maybe at most four hundred, there is nothing else to say, so it is time

---

to close it down. I knew *The Autobiography of Miss Jane Pittman* would cover a hundred years and that it would be a longer novel than my earlier ones. I have been influenced by so many different forms of writing. I studied Greek tragedy at San Francisco State, and I've always thought the idea of having things in a single setting and limited to twenty-four hours was the ideal way of telling stories. For example, "A Long Day in November" takes place within less than twenty-four hours, as do "Bloodline" and "The Sky Is Gray." "Just Like a Tree" takes place in three hours. It's all concentrated. *The Autobiography of Miss Jane* was a different thing altogether.

Interviewer: Jefferson's notebook is one of the most moving parts of *A Lesson Before Dying*. You get inside his head, but as readers, we know Grant doesn't get the notebook until the end. It is powerful not only because of its content, but also because the reader sees the diary before Grant receives it. How did you decide on the placement of the diary?

Gaines: I did it so it would work chronologically with the rest of the novel. That book has been translated into German, and they moved the notebook chapter to the end. I thought it should be before the end, so you would still see Jefferson after he dies, after Grant is given the notebook. I've sold the rights to HBO. They are supposed to start shooting it in October of '98. I have no idea what they are going to do with it or where they are going to film it. It has also been adapted as a play for the Alabama Shakespeare Company.

Interviewer: The novel is cinematic in the same way Tolstoy's "The Death of Ivan Ilyich" is. The reader sees every movement of the characters as if they are on a stage.

Gaines: One of the things I learned from Turgenev's *Fathers and Sons* is that something is always happening in one setting, then you move on to something else. If you look at the chapters in that novel, I don't think any one is longer or shorter than the others. I wrote a rough draft every week and then went over it. They would always end up the same number of pages. I had to write that book over a period of seven years, writing only half the year because I was teaching at USL. I would go back to San Francisco at the end of December and start in late January, writing until the end of July, when I was ready to come back to Lafayette and teach. *A Lesson Before Dying* is the only novel I've ever written that way, and it really scared me because I didn't know how I would go back to it the first time I put it aside for six months. I was afraid the reader would see those breaks, so I worked on smoothing them out. It may have been good because if the novel had been written in three years, I might not have had as many different elements coming into the story. I don't know if I would have had the notebook in the story. But because I was thinking about it over a period of seven years, those things just came into it.

Interviewer: You received a lot of publicity when Oprah Winfrey chose *A Lesson Before Dying* for her book club. How did you feel when you learned this?

Gaines: She called me personally, and I didn't believe it was her. I had met her when the book first came out. She said, "We've chosen *A Lesson Before Dying* for the Oprah Book Club. This is all hush-hush until I announce it on my show." I said, "It's okay with me, just as long as I can tell my wife." She came to Louisiana, to the plantation at False River. We spent two days together.

Interviewer: The novel had already drawn attention when it won the National Book Critics Circle Award in 1993. Did you feel a rush of new readership because of Oprah's influence?

Gaines: Oh, yes. Before, the book was selling well, but it was selling to high schools and libraries. With Oprah, it sold to the general public. There were between 800,000 and a million copies printed as soon as she announced it. Everybody knew *The Autobiography of Miss Jane Pittman*, but they never knew who wrote it. Now they know Ernest Gaines wrote *A Lesson Before Dying* because they saw me on the show. I receive many letters from people all over the country and different parts of the world, and most of them are coming from white, probably middle-aged males. It's the first time I've received letters from this particular group. Bill Gates said *A Lesson Before Dying* was one of his favorite books, along with *The Catcher in the Rye*. That's good to hear, but he never sent me any computer stuff. I've always received many letters from students, but it seems *A Lesson Before Dying* has touched a lot of people.

Interviewer: How do you feel about all the attention?

Gaines: I'm happy people are reading the book, but other than that, I just do the same thing. I teach. My wife and I still go to the same restaurants. We still visit our friends, things like that.

"You try not to answer things but to perk the interest or the intellect of the reader."

Interviewer: Many people believe *The Autobiography of Miss Jane Pittman* is an autobiography with an introduction by Ernest J. Gaines.

Gaines: Several people reviewed it as an autobiography, and many bookstores keep it on the autobiography shelf. There was a very famous magazine in New York that called me for a picture of Miss Jane because they were reviewing the book. I said, "You know, that is a fictitious character." They said, "Oh, my God!" They had already written the review, and they wanted a picture to go with it. Once I was in Orlando, Florida, talking to some people, and a guy said, "Mr. Gaines, may I ask you a question? How long did you have to interview that old lady before you had enough material to write the book?"

Interviewer: What do you feel is your responsibility as a novelist?

Gaines: You try to not answer things but to perk the interest or the intellect of the reader and let him ask questions. Once the reader begins to ask these questions, he will get some answers that will lead him to other things so he can discuss it with other people. I don't know how to give answers, and I tell my students that. I try to create characters who develop through the course of the novel, characters who will learn and grow before they die, and from whom the reader can learn and grow.

REUNION / *Susan Terris*

Yesterday, my sister, her voice crackling across
2000 miles, phoned to say the counselors
of our old summer camp have invited us to
a reunion tea. *Frosty,* she told me,
will be there. Huck and Nan.
Also Sparky, Jo, and C.G. Math may not be
my strong suit, but even I can compute
the counselors we last saw 40 years ago
are filing Medicare forms, collecting
Social Security. These women who loved
other women passionately and young girls
with chaste restraint, discarding guitars,
Levis worn beltless on their hips, and Pendletons
with Camels in their pockets, will be
crooking handbags and patting wiry curls.

Is Marge coming? I asked and what would we
all discuss as we crumbled macaroons?
Our husbands, their partners? Our children,
their pets? Our Milosz, their Kahlil Gibran?
Even as my sister and I jammed the line
with jests, I felt shamed and ashamed by
my condescension. So I said I was cooking supper
and hung up. Then, chopping leeks, I wept
knowing I'd loved these women because they
gazed past 12, past 14, past 16.
Yet, still, I can't forgive them for striding
from old photos to reandrogynize me, so I rang
my sister back and said I couldn't afford to come.

TWELVE: ROUGH AND UNSUGARED /
Susan Terris

River time was the only time
as we relished what was stolen, what was
borrowed and the pleasure in each.
Past sandbanks on the Flambeau,
adrenaline high, we whitewatered
in canvas canoes, buoyed by
the weightlessness of youth where
risks were taken, not subjects to
debate. At night, the campfire flared

and, with our counselor, we bellied
between furrows, stole armfuls
of corn to roast for supper.
But we'd forgotten to portage salt,
so we scrubbed our faces, tucked shirttails,
hiked to the farmhouse by the field
where we—well-mannered thieves—
asked to borrow, even dug in pockets
and offered to pay.

Later, squatting by flames to fend off
mosquito and bear, we roasted our booty,
lavished charred grains with pinches
of salt, knowing it was horse corn—
feed for stock, rough and unsugared.
But we filled our stomachs,
picked our teeth, smelled wet cobs,
our gamy, high-breasted bodies dimly
aware, as we listened to fugue of

guitar and wave, how the river had
spun us free, and what was stolen had
sweetness too complex for the tongue.

THIRTEEN: THE IRON HANDLE OF INNISFREE / *Susan Terris*

Innisfree: not the bee-wattled glade of Yeats
but Wisconsin by fast-moving water.
Our tents were up. Dinner was squaw corn
and Ritz apple pie from the campfire oven.
And that night, before the bear came,
my counselor—careful not to touch her body
to mine—leaned toward me under inked pines
and kissed me full on the lips.

Later, after the bear, after morning coffee
with eggshells, we swam the white river across
from Innisfree; and as we—naiads on boulders
ringed by water—lounged, I found the handle,
a heavy iron oval, its shaft sunk deep into rock.
Open sesame, I told myself. With a twist,

hidden places might be revealed. As my counselor
eyed me in my two-piece cotton suit,
I took hold of the handle and slipped into the river,
held fast and twisting, tethered yet free.
Then, without looking back, I uncurled my fingers
and let the current fly me downstream
away from rock, iron, flesh: elements that
beggared revelation.

FOURTEEN: BEDTIME STORY / *Susan Terris*

My last year as a camper, last trip on the Flowage.
After weeks of rain, mosquitoes smudging
the air in pewter clouds, we fled to our tents
after dinner. A terrible end for a terrible day:
we'd dinged a canoe, forgotten coffee, and
my cabinmates were furious I'd been chosen.
Next summer, I'd be staff—
a JC—while they were still campers.

Taunting, they made me tent with our counselor
Marge, said I was in love with her.
To escape girls and mosquitoes, Marge and I
zippered in. It was hot and sunset,
through netting, a crosshatch of amber
as we stripped to underwear, lay on sleeping bags,
and gazed out. Then Marge, cameo Marge
with the gray-marble eyes, said she'd rub

my back, began to knead muscles, whispering,
Splenius, deltoid, trapezius, exterior oblique,
gluteus . . . Each Latin word offered
in flat Wisconsin tones, each touch tender
yet noninvasive. Lying there, I drifted,
watched the sky now amethyst bleeding onyx,
trying to slough off the day, unwilling to admit
a woman was making love to my back.

FIFTEEN: RUNNING GOOSE-EYE/
Susan Terris

Goose-Eye the unrunnable rapid.
I faced it three times in one day. Though canoes were
supposed to be on lead lines while
we waded the shallow chute near shore,
water was raging over our heads
and Jen, my co-counselor, spiking a fever,
was incoherent. So I asked the girls to
bushwhack the woods to the low eddies.
Then with my cousin as bow
and Jen athwart as dead weight, I knifed
canoes one by one through Goose-Eye.

Wet and crazed, sweeping by rocks and holes,
buoyed by shouts from the girls below,
I claimed the river. Downstream—
a road and a phone and I called camp, said
we'd run Goose-Eye three times, said Jen
was sick and we needed a blue-truck pickup.
Marge came, yet when I slid into
the truck and reached out,
she pulled away, frowned as if I'd grown
too old and too bold. But the campers
lined the road as we rattled in,

cheering, calling my name. Alive then,
drenched with pleasure, I thought risk-taking
made me immortal. Was this ardor tamped
by conscience? I'd like to say yes,
but it wasn't. Even today, it shivers me
to recall how I rose three times up from
the whitewater of the Chippewa and flew.

SIXTEEN: TOLLING THE BELL / *Susan Terris*

Midnight: straddling the roof under a half-moon,
we pulled the rope and rang each time a car
peeled in. The campers and their trunks of
sooty clothes were gone. Now Marge, Jen,
and the others straggled back as we—
JCs too young for bars in town—were
gabled there drinking pop, watching them.

P.E. teachers in their 20s, they weren't like us,
though we'd frayed jeans and spit-combed
ducktails like theirs. Especially Marge's.
We envied her blondness, real, we knew,
since communal showers showed pubic hair
gold as curls on her head. She said she'd never
marry or have kids, though her mother
held out hope. Marge—my sister learned
at the reunion—died of breast cancer at 33.

Marge's breasts: dark-nippled globes
with blue veins that pitched when she bent
to razor hair on her legs. But that August night,
Marge and Jen climbed from a Chevy coupe
and linked arms, their moon-shadows
stilting into pine-needled dark. Wistful,
I thought of Goose-Eye, Innisfree,
of stealing corn, sharing tents. Then I
tolled the bell again for friends on the way to
becoming strangers, women whose lives had,
for a while, grafted a subtle rhythm onto mine.

Susan Terris is a Larry Levis Editors' Prize finalist. She has published a number of poetry collections, including *Curved Space.*

A YANKEES FAN IN THE FLOATING WORLD/*Melanie Hammer*

WHILE I WAS AWAY at college, my parents bought and sold a couple of houses and changed their address three times, covering a distance of several hundred miles. By the time I graduated and moved back in with them, they were living on the twenty-ninth floor of a high-rise in midtown Manhattan. They'd taken a two-bedroom apartment, partly because of the significant expense involved if they went for something larger, but also as if they knew in advance that once the children went off to college none of them would ever come back to stay long. Both of my brothers had a couple of years to go at school, so there was maneuvering room. We staked out territory, my father occupying my parents' bedroom, my mother the living room, I the spare bedroom.

I had majored in English, but it turned out to be even more useful that I had excelled at typing in junior high. I landed a job as an editorial assistant at a university press and set about the business of becoming a grown-up. My two bosses treated me as if I were bright enough, one in particular reminding me that she had started off as an editorial assistant herself. They acquired books, and I typed their correspondence with a variety of authors. They had interesting jobs, but I liked it better over in copyediting, a warren where women in glasses polished text like old silver, working in the intricacies of language until they brought it to a shine. There was a woman I liked particularly, with silvery blond hair and silvery blue eyes. She lived quietly by herself on Long Island and commuted to work every day on the train. In my head, I filed her away as someone I might grow up to be much later. Meanwhile, I wasn't staying. I took a paycheck every two weeks and put most of it away. For the moment I didn't want to be much of anything, and couldn't imagine that I ever would.

In April I took my first sick day to go to Opening Day at Yankee Stadium. During two years of remodeling, the Yankees had shared Shea Stadium with the Mets, but now they were coming back to the Bronx. I left the apartment a little after nine. The game was a sellout, but bleacher tickets were going on sale at eleven.

The 4 train runs underground up the East Side of Manhattan and into the Bronx, but at Yankee Stadium it rises out of the tunnel onto elevated tracks. That morning we burst into sunshine, and I could look into the stadium and see the differences. The view-blocking pillars were gone, and the blue of the seats was brighter. I stood on the platform for a moment, as people swirled around me, and waited while the train pulled out and I got another view of the stadium. I could see that the old façade had been pulled down, painted white, and made into trim in the outfield. I'd been away a long time.

The grass stretched out unblemished in front of the bleachers. The fences had been pulled in; the monuments, which had been a center fielder's nightmare, were back behind the fence. Despite the changes, however, there was more the same than different: the green grass mowed into a grid of interlocking rectangles, the foul lines and batters' boxes lined bright white against the dirt, the large, clean diamond laid out on the ground. For the first time, I felt like I'd come home from school.

Looking at the mostly unfamiliar names on the scorecard, I found out that the new young second baseman, Willie Randolph, was three months shy of his twenty-second birthday. I was three weeks older. I sat in the bleachers, watching batting practice, watching Randolph, number 30. All my life, I'd been used to thinking of ballplayers as grownups, myself as a kid, but that afternoon in Yankee Stadium, I realized that I was catching up to them. They'd solved the mystery, it seemed to me, of how to be, stumbled into it, or looked inside themselves and found it, or been tapped on the shoulder. They were able to go forward, not just because they were good at something but because they were able to devote themselves. Years later, I'd read an interview in which Randolph said that growing up, he hadn't been the most talented player in his neighborhood, Bushwick, in Brooklyn, but he'd been one of the few to stay with it, work at it. But that afternoon I watched Willie Randolph take ground balls and shook my head. It was too hard a puzzle for me. I was just there to watch a baseball game.

With most of my old friends still away at school, I explored relations with my fellow editorial assistants. Some of the young women I hung around with were just passing through, too, bound back to Howard or Dartmouth when their publishing internships were over. Elaine Weissberg, though, was there for the long term. Elaine was very thin and favored baggy clothes that were too young for her, like big jumpers over blouses with Peter Pan collars carefully buttoned to the neck. I hadn't yet known anyone with the big knees of anorexics, but I suspected Elaine was hiding, or hiding something under her clothes. She lived about twenty blocks south of my parents' apartment and had converted a closet into a darkroom. Her pictures were posted all over her walls. There was a hairstylist on Elaine's block, and there was a particular mannequin head in the window that was always being restyled. Elaine kept tabs on the mannequin, named her Justine, and photographed her short, dark, smooth, long, blond, curly, and every permutation in between. Elaine shot in black and white and then took special crayons to her pictures, touching up the lips, or the skin, or shadowing the eyes, or leaving colored marks in places that looked random. Elaine herself never wore makeup, and her light brown hair was always blunt cut around her jaw, carefully styleless. I loved the Justine series. I didn't quite know what Elaine was getting at with it, but I knew enough to recognize, watching Elaine with her camera, a person absorbed in her work, givig herself to it wholeheartedly. elaine didn't talk much about herself, but from Justine she held nothing back.

If there was anything I was capable of feeling committed to, it was the Yankees. I could bribe no one I knew into going to the stadium with me, and once a week or so, when the Yankees were home, I'd sit by myself in the upper deck, frequently, in April and early May, in two or three sweaters. I'd eat ice cream, pretending it was summer already, and watch the game play out on the field below me. If I was lonely, I didn't know it. I watched Thurman Munson control the game from behind the plate, Billy Martin kick dirt on umpires, Catfish Hunter give up some of the biggest home runs I'd ever seen, almost always in early innings with nobody on, then settle down and make the opposition look feeble for the rest of the game. Baseball had changed in some ways from when I was a kid: they had the designated hitter in the American League; it spared fans both the spectacle of the pitcher hitting and the intricacies of baseball strategy, which I missed. It tipped the balance toward hitting, and I had always preferred a good 1-0 or 2-1 pitchers' duel. They had divisional play, which meant a team could have the best record across the 162-game season and still not make it to the World Series. I was used to thinking of myself as a rebel, but when it came to baseball, I was a traditionalist. Fortunately, the Yankees also retained one player from my childhood, Roy White—a quick, switch-hitting outfielder with a pigeon-toed stance—and that helped ease me through the changes. Despite the alterations, baseball still rested on a foundation of well-executed fundamentals: hitting the cutoff man, taking the extra base, throwing a first strike to a hitter. I sat in the upper deck, suspended above the field, and looked down like one waiting for mysteries to be revealed.

At the beginning of September, I had enough money. I gave notice at work, bought a round-trip ticket on Icelandic Airlines where the return half would be good for a year, and invested in a warm sleeping bag and a backpack. I had thrown over a promising job, and my father refused to give his blessing to my trip, but the only thing I regretted was the Yankees, who looked like they would be winning the American League East, and possibly their first pennant since 1964. If I left town, I'd miss it, but I couldn't hang around any longer inside my own skin. I had to get out.

Once in Europe, I traveled hard every day, as if I feared entire countries would fold up their tents and disappear before I could get there. Gradually, I slowed down. Except for minimal traveler's talk for food, youth hostel lodgings, train schedules, I went days without saying a word to anyone. I was the only person in the girls' side of youth hostels in some of the smaller towns in Belgium; I walked the streets wrapped in the comforting solitude that comes from knowing I'd recognize no face, no street corner, and, in the Flemish part of the country, not even a spoken word. My time was my own; I ate and slept according to my own whims, modified by the youth hostels' rules. If I arrived somewhere and decided I didn't like it at first or second glance, I went someplace else immediately. Every day I wandered strange cities, admiring their art, their buildings, their monuments, their town squares. I ate their food, french fries wrapped in white paper cones, crepes from a street corner, coffee in small bowls.

I never read a newspaper or listened to a radio. I wondered about the Yankees now and then, but mostly it was as if the world I had left had ceased to exist. Behind the everyday sensations, though, a kind of clock had started ticking in my head. If I'd gone to Europe to find myself, or at least someone who looked familiar, I'd better get to it.

The farther north I went, the grayer the skies became. On my last day in London, in early October, it started to rain, and it continued to rain almost every day while I made my way up through England and into Scotland. In Edinburgh, I woke up with a throat so sore I could hardly swallow, and found my way to the local hospital. The doctor checked me out, said it was just a bad cold, recommended staying indoors and drinking lots of liquids for a day or two. When I asked how to pay the bill, he explained the concept of socialized medicine. I had my thumb out again by afternoon. I felt lousy, but it was worse if I stayed in one place.

It took nearly a month to loop through Scotland, Ireland, Wales and back to London, where there was a thick packet of mail waiting for me at the American Express office. Standing there with the stack of U.S. postmarks, I suddenly realized the World Series was over. I sorted through the envelopes, finally pausing at a fat one addressed to me by my father. I slit it open, and there, neatly batched by game, continuations of articles stapled together, were three New York papers' coverage of the 1976 World Series. The Yankees had lost to the Big Red Machine in four straight, but I read through anyway, drinking tea and trying to stay warm. One of the reporters had asked Reds manager Sparky Anderson how Thurman Munson stacked up against Johnny Bench, the Reds' future Hall-of-Fame catcher, and Sparky had said that he wouldn't want to embarrass anyone by comparing them with Johnny Bench. But Thurm wasn't just anyone, and I felt a wave of righteous anger on his behalf, along with something else that just might have been homesickness.

Athens was where I was when I had less than fifty dollars in my pocket, and, according to a rule I'd set myself, that was the place where I looked for work. I cashed in the return half of my plane ticket for another seventy-five dollars and tried to orient myself. In the Athens youth hostel there was another young woman about my age, with long blond hair, an unfinished MA in architecture, and a kind of grim look around the mouth. She wasn't going home either. Margaret spoke enough Greek that we were able to negotiate ourselves a basement apartment for forty dollars a month. I got work teaching English to two little girls, six days a week after school, and she got work cleaning house for the family of an American ex-astronaut who had once walked on the moon. In that basement apartment, with linoleum covering the water-stained walls, where the toilet made such strange noises we decided it was talking and named it Theobald, we hunkered down and saved our money. If Athens wore thin after a while, it didn't matter; it was a cheap city to live in. We devoted ourselves to small pleasures: the libaray at the Hellenic-American Center; an occasional movie; the stupid deaths and dowry scams in the *Athens Daily News*. We were going to travel more, as much as we wanted, and we wouldn't go home until we were ready, whenever that was.

One October afternoon a little over a year from the day I'd left, I was standing in a small shop in the Plaka, that area of old, narrow streets and shops crunched at the foot of the Acropolis. I had enough money to travel for a few more months, but I'd be going home after that. The family I was looking to buy presents for I hadn't seen in over a year. Considering the sweaters in the store, trying to think what my two brothers, my mother and father might like, I realized I was still inside my own skin. I'd lived on my own in a foreign country, I'd walked streets I'd previously only read or dreamed about, but if those experiences had changed me in any fundamental way, I had yet to see how. I hadn't expected a clear signpost, but with all the time I'd had to look inward, I'd have thought I would have gotten at least a hint as to what direction to take. Instead, I was going home, as far as I could tell, almost exactly the same person I had been when I left.

I had my hand on a navy-blue cable sweater that might work for my brother Mike when the language on the radio station the shopkeeper had been playing finally penetrated my consciousness. English. It was the American Armed Forces Network, broadcasting the last game of the 1977 World Series between the Yankees and the Dodgers.

". . . Reggie Jackson," the announcer was saying. "Jackson has two home runs already in this game."

I stood still, listening to the call. Then I heard the familiar "tock," the radio-filtered sound of a bat solidly hitting a ball. Reggie Jackson had hit three home runs in one World Series game, the first time it had ever been done. I hardly thought of Reggie as a Yankee, he was such a recent acquisition, but he was wearing a Yankees uniform, and the Yankees were winning. I looked out into the winding streets of the Plaka, my head full of the buzz of a stadium crowd and the announcers' excited voices. For the first time in a year and a half, I could hear home calling me.

Melanie Hammer is a finalist in the Editors' Prize contest. Her work has appeared previously in numerous journals.

THE CHOSEN/*Steve Adams*

ONE HAS TO PONDER what he felt as he watched it fall from the sky, a dark spot that materialized from nowhere against endless pale blue. As moment by moment it increased in size, there was nothing to do but accept, because he knew it would somehow miss the entire Sea of Japan and strike and sink the small speck upon the water where he stood. That's what he told the police afterward. What he was not prepared for was the object itself—a rather stout and full-grown horse.

When they retrieved the boat it looked like someone had dropped a boulder through its wooden deck that had passed clear through its hull. His men said their boss refused to leave the hole at the time, seemed to want nothing more than to watch the sea rise through it. And as the boat foundered and his men jumped into the water and struggled to the odd assortment of life preservers flung quite far from the boat by an overzealous young fish scaler, they spotted their boss, Takashi Fumiyama, floating some thirty yards away, clinging to the equine corpse, its bones turned to meal but its body providing a more-than-satisfactory life raft.

J. Thomas Foxbourne III, claims adjuster at the Tokyo branch of Lloyd's of London, kept flipping through the pages of the document on his desk as if he were missing something, as if it were only a matter of staring long enough at the right page for the entire matter to clarify. The text of the document, however, continued to fight logic. Nevertheless, the information was, he had to admit, complete. A Mr. Sozo Ishido owned the policy and had filed a claim for a Mr. Takashi Fumiyama. Mr. Fumiyama's fishing boat was sunk when a horse fell out of the sky and crashed through it. The policy was specifically written to cover "Acts of God." As usual, the Japanese police were meticulous. According to their report, the impression of a horse-sized object upon the ship was unmistakable. Mr. Fumiyama even had "said horse" in possession upon rescue.

Various hypotheses regarding the event had been proffered—in writing, to Mr. Foxbourne's astonishment. He was not a believer in the maxim that no idea was too stupid to be spoken, let alone committed to the permanency of ink and paper.

1. *The horse was standing on the edge of a bluff overlooking the ocean. Something behind the creature startled it and it leapt off. At that very moment a waterspout formed under it, which carried it out to sea and flung it high into the sky, where it eventually fell and sank the fisherman's boat.*
2. *A yacht was sailing in the vicinity. The horse was standing on deck, likely the top deck. An exceptionally strong gust of wind lifted the horse from the ship and carried it over Mr. Fumiyama's boat.*
3. *The horse didn't fall from the sky at all. It rose from the sea. The horse could have been swimming in the ocean, where it was caught in a very powerful undertow and pulled into one of Japan's notoriously strong underwater currents. The day of the accident, an underwater earthquake registered in the East China Sea. That geological disturbance could have created a temporary crosscurrent that battled the primary current, creating an underwater explosion of sorts that hoisted the horse into the air above the boat. Likely there were fish falling from the sky at the time as well. This detail would be worth looking into.*
4. *Check on third-world space programs.*

Foxbourne considered that the horse might have just as easily built itself a set of wings of wax and feathers, then flown too near the sun. He pushed the document aside and shook his head. Number 4 was the only entry that seemed not entirely driven by lunatic fantasies. But its tone, brevity and concept indicated that its author was at least half jesting, and Foxbourne did not appreciate tomfoolery in documents where the firm stood to lose money. He also had no doubt that among the fishermen and "'simple peasant folk" the story was already becoming legend, something along the lines of an angry sea god/dess sending the horse as a sign of the coming Apocalypse. That sort of blather.

Foxbourne shook his head. This case was not a difficult one. In fact it was very simple. He picked up a pencil and scrawled along the bottom of the sheet:

5. *Takashi Fumiyama is a liar.*

Foxbourne had to admit a general disappointment with the Japanese. From afar they'd always seemed (in his own words) "the most British of the Asians." He adored the British; in fact, he affected a bit of an accent, as did many of his chums in the Yale Glee Club. Never mind that Foxbourne was from New Jersey. "Princeton," he would correct. "I'm from

Princeton, and Princeton is *not* New Jersey." It might not have been, but it certainly was *in* New Jersey, which was one of several deciding factors in his accepting Yale over Princeton. New Jersey steps up to Connecticut, and Connecticut seemed to him the closest the United States ever came to Britain.

After graduation he'd taken this position knowing he could have immediately gotten a higher one elsewhere, but not with as prominent a company. "Start with the top, and stay with the top," he was fond of saying. A year or two in the field should put him on the fast track and hopefully take him to Lloyd's of London in London itself. But his Japanese was sadly lacking. He'd not even gotten past such basics as, "Thank you very much" or, "Hello, how are you?" Languages were not his strength, he told himself. Numbers were, and a capacity to make order out of confusion, as well as the boldness to call a spade a spade.

Fortunately, Japanese businessmen spoke proper English (the language of business, he noted proudly), and he was able to transact almost all affairs without pulling out his English-Japanese dictionary. But the moment his Japanese associates dropped into their native tongue, Foxbourne worried that he was being conspired against. When they broke into laughter, as they often did, then turned and smiled knowingly at him, Foxbourne was certain he was the butt of some joke. Was his fly open? Was soup on his tie?

They aggravated him to no end at meetings, saying little to nothing, allowing him to ramble on and on; all the while they smiled agreeably. And Foxbourne, usually the very model of restraint, had on more than one occasion said more than he should have. He still cringed remembering the time he had launched into a lecture regarding the discipline, organizational skills and all-around spirit of the British.

Before he could stop himself he was carrying on about "how bravely the Brits comported themselves during World War II," when he realized his gaffe and stopped in midsentence. His words seemed to float as visibly as brightly colored balloons. And still they smiled, nodded, superior and forgiving as the Buddha.

Then there was this medieval sense of honor they clung to. Hadn't they read their own newspapers? Hadn't they gone through a banking scandal? Or two, or three? And above all, he still couldn't make himself believe, as he'd been informed during orientation, that the word "no" was almost never heard in Japanese because to speak it was considered the height of rudeness. He was a claims adjuster, after all. Wasn't it his job to say "no"? How can you do business if you can't say "no"? On the page below where he'd written "Takashi Fumiyama is a liar," he wrote the word "no" ten times in a neat, ordered row.

Kim, a slight, lovely young woman, had spent two years in the U.S. pursuing her MBA from Rutgers. For that reason the higher powers at Lloyd's-Tokyo had paired her with Foxbourne in the hope that she could, with her experience in America, help him make the apparently difficult transition into their culture. The two were learning from the ground floor up. Both were expected to go far.

Foxbourne asked her to check on the policy holder, Mr. Ishido, but she already had the answer. He was a big businessman who owned a fleet of over 500 fishing boats. Fumiyama was his brother-in-law, to whom he'd given the boat as a wedding gift. Mr. Ishido had insured the boat with the rest of his fleet out of respect for his deceased sister, Fumiyama's wife, and also because he genuinely cared for the fisherman. "He told me," she said, "that his brother-in-law might not always have both feet on the ground, but that he was an honorable man."

The way she said "honorable man . . ." Again, Foxbourne was being asked to read between the lines. "Just because he's an honorable man doesn't mean he isn't a liar. Let's go."

Kim drove the few hours it took them to cross the island to Niigata, just south of Fumiyama's home. While Foxbourne felt sharp, keen, excited about exposing the scoundrel, Kim remained taciturn. He tried to change her mood by asking about Rutgers' football team. He admitted that they beat Yale's year in, year out. But rugby . . . that was a different slice of pie. A man's game, that was! As often happened on this other side of the world, though, Foxbourne ended up talking only to himself.

"Why would he lie?" Kim finally said when they reached Niigata.

"For the money, of course."

"But a liar would make up a much more likely story than a horse falling from the sky."

"Maybe he's a very clever liar. Maybe he came up with a story so outrageous he thought no one would dare challenge him. He could have brought the horse on board, had his men saw through the boat, paid everyone off. It's not that far-fetched. Certainly not as far-fetched as his story."

They drove the rest of the way in silence. Fumiyama lived fifteen miles north of the city, along the coast. As they stopped and walked up to the fisherman's tiny, box-shaped house, the air was redolent with the salt and life of the ocean. For a brief moment Foxbourne recalled the Jersey shore when he was a kid, then quickly shook the memory from his mind because Fumiyama, a short, round, bald man stood at his door.

Kim and Fumiyama bowed and exchanged greetings in Japanese. Foxbourne reached out and shook the fisherman's hand.

In the entrance to the house, Kim slipped out of her shoes, then she and Fumiyama stood patiently while Foxbourne yanked at a knot in his right shoelace. Finally Foxbourne wrenched the shoe off, tied knot and all, and joined Kim and Fumiyama.

Fumiyama served tea then Foxbourne listened to the two of them jabber for more than thirty minutes. Kim pretended that Foxbourne was somehow involved in the conversation, telling him an occasional detail the fisherman shared, such as, "Mr. Fumiyama thinks Madonna is a very dynamic performer," upon which news Foxbourne smiled and nodded with the enthusiasm of a bobbing-head doll. Then back to the native tongue. The laughter. The smiles in his direction. As Foxbourne sat on his tiny chair, his feet exposed, his hands between his knees, forcing smile after smile, he suffered an almost unbearable urge to run screaming through the rice-paper panels separating the rooms in the house. What, after all, was Kim's problem? Someone would have to discuss the concept of "cutting to the chase" with her.

At last Kim and Fumiyama rose. "I have a few questions to ask him," Foxbourne blurted out.

"Yes. But first Mr. Fumiyama would like to show you something." On that she turned and followed Fumiyama. Frustrated, Foxbourne tagged along after them, stooping beneath the low ceiling in the hall.

Fumiyama turned to them and smiled, pulled open a sliding panel and motioned them to step into a dark room lit by close to a hundred candles. He followed them inside, then closed the panel behind them. Incense drifted visibly through the air. At the end of the room on a small stage—pulpit, because there was no doubt Foxbourne had staggered into a church—stood the horse in question. One of the finest jobs of taxidermy Foxbourne had ever seen, he had to admit.

At first glance he recalled Trigger, Roy Rogers' lifelong companion stuffed like some trophy bass in the Roy Rogers Museum, but that comparison didn't seem accurate because what stood before him now was art; gave grace, reverence, to the essence of the creature that had fallen from the sky. The short chestnut horse was not a thoroughbred. It had a broad rump, a little bit of belly, a little fat from comfort and long days of nothing but eating and standing in sunlight. It stood turned, slightly angled in a fastidiously rendered setting with long yellow grass before a sky-blue backdrop, and looked over its shoulder. Looked a degree . . . upward.

"What did you think of Mr. Fumiyama?" Kim asked during the drive back.

Whatever limitations Foxbourne suffered, stupidity and stubbornness were not on the short list. Upon seeing the shrine Foxbourne had known immediately that Fumiyama was no liar. Kim's indirectness about the affair irritated him. Why couldn't she just come out and say she was right, he was wrong? "I think it's quite likely," he said, "that Mr. Fumiyama is telling the truth."

"I think you may be right," she said, as if it were the first time the possibility had crossed her mind, as if she'd been one step from throwing the transgressor to the hounds but had now been swayed by Foxbourne's sound reasoning. This charade aggravated Foxbourne. She'd bested him. She had a right to a good gloat. Meanwhile, his mind was skimming over that list of absurd possible explanations for the horse, and like a bee to the proper flower, it landed on number 4: "Check on third-world space programs." Which, of course, was ridiculous but nevertheless pointed in the right direction.

"Maybe we pay him now?" Kim said.

"Pay him?"

"If we are both certain he is not lying, we could pay for the boat and sign off on it."

"That would be admitting defeat."

"For who?" she said, a trace of irritation showing.

"For reason."

"Reason seems at this point a waste of time, a waste of billable hours. Mr. Fumiyama doesn't need reason. In fact, he said the whole experience transformed his life."

"It's a question of integrity. We need an answer here, unless you wish to conclude that Jehovah threw the horse down from on high as a personal religious marker to that peasant."

"Perhaps he did," she said, flushed with anger.

That's her exposure to the U.S. of A., thought Foxbourne. He preferred her that way, preferred a woman with spirit! Best to mollify her a degree. "I didn't mean that 'peasant' comment the way it sounded," he told her. "I should have said 'blue collar.' Working man. Salt of the earth. Backbone of industry. I've nothing but respect for the working man."

She shook her head. "That 'working man' needs a new boat very soon. If you must find an explanation for this event, then I will help you to find it. But if it takes very long, I recommend we accept the possibility of divine providence. An 'Act of God,' as the policy states, Mr. Fumiyama was fully protected against."

Foxbourne kept quiet but squirmed in his seat, considering the prospect of any case he worked on going unresolved. But this one in particular would appear a joke and, unsolved, might well follow him throughout his career. A horse fell from the sky and sank a boat at sea? And he *paid* on it, writing it off as a sacred act of the Holy? No, for the sake of his career—for the sake of Kim's—he could not give up, would not give in to the forces of anarchy and mysticism. This case, perhaps more than any other he might ever come across, could define his career, and therefore must be solved, and solved completely.

Musings on the religious were uncharted territory for Foxbourne. Though he considered himself agnostic, it gave him the willies to imagine such a theology, the implications of a deity who would pull such a stunt. Was he supposed to accept that God himself, father of Christ Our Lord, was a vaudevillian, Master of the Banana Peel Pratfall? Not if Foxbourne had any say in the matter. Number 4 on his list pointed Foxbourne's eyes upward, as had the gaze of the horse on the altar.

The explanation was very simple, of course. Not as simple as he'd first surmised, but still simple enough. So Foxbourne, having arrived at his answer once again, worked backward to prove it. He procured a map of the Sea of Japan and marked an X where the boat was sunk. He located the airports of the largest Japanese cities and drew a line from them through the X. Foxbourne studied the map. By far the most likely culprits were the Chinese, the Koreans and the Russians. Which, he asked himself, according to his prejudices and gut instincts, would be more likely to lose a horse out its cargo door? "The bloody Russians, of course," he answered aloud.

Soon he and Kim were calling the major airports, talking to customs officials, checking air-traffic-control records. Nothing. Kim tracked down all the midlevel airports, and they went through the same paces with the same results. After another full day of phone calls and chasing leads, an official at a tiny airstrip near Sendai told them that a Russian cargo plane had landed there on the day in question, but he was certain no livestock was involved. "It makes no sense to fly livestock," the man said. "Too expensive." When pressed about what the plane was transporting, the man admitted it was bringing in a shipment of vodka, along with boxes of old propaganda buttons and posters from Communist Russia. "Very popular with the kids," he explained. These items were being exchanged for a variety of goods, mostly secondhand electronics—old radios, televisions, a few antiquated computers—with a Japanese merchant by the name of Mako Iko. "All legal," the official quickly assured Kim. "All checked out." He was hesitant to give the merchant's phone number but acquiesced when Kim mentioned that there was stolen property involved and perhaps he would rather give the merchant's number to the police.

Foxbourne leaned back in his chair, ever so gratified with his instincts. Yes, he and Kim had spent two full work days pinning this matter down, and some would question the time charged back to the company, but a good claims adjuster must never rest, must turn over every leaf, look under every rock, until each issue in question was resolved.

He had a sudden urge to smoke a cigar, though he'd never smoked one in his life. He looked at his watch. "Kim, it's after five. What say we knock off and call this 'blackguard' first thing in the morning when he's more likely to be in his office? And why don't you let me treat you to dinner for all your terrific work. Restaurant of your choice." Foxbourne was in such good spirits that he was even considering trying sushi for the first time. When in Rome, after all! But Kim respectfully declined, said she still had work to do on another case and would need to stay in the office for hours. Not letting himself be disappointed, he took himself out to a fine meal of chicken teriyaki and shrimp tempura.

Foxbourne sat at the edge of his seat leaning toward Kim, his hands clasped before him. "What's he saying?"

Kim held up her hand to silence him a moment, then began translating what she was hearing. "After the cargo was nearly loaded—all legal, he says—one of the Russians, Igor, the drunk one, saw a horse wandering untethered, unclaimed . . . apparently unowned, less than fifty feet away. Mr. Iko says that before he knew what was happening, Igor, the drunk one, was leading the horse up the loading ramp into the plane." Kim spoke Japanese into the phone for a moment, nodded, then turned to Foxbourne. "Mr. Iko said he tried to stop him, but 'how can you stop a drunk Russian?' He said he tried to reason with the drunk one's coworkers, but—in his own words again—'how can you reason with Russians?' So the plane took off with the cargo of electronics equipment and one kidnapped, untethered horse—over the very loud protestations of Mr. Iko."

Foxbourne smiled, then looked out the window contentedly.

The rest was easy—having one of Lloyd's Russian speakers contact the pilot of the plane. In the ensuing report the pilot stated that as they were reaching cruising altitude, the horse suddenly "went crazy," running up and down the hull of the airplane, bucking and kicking at the walls, until "that idiot, Igor" pulled open the cargo door and the horse leaped out. To make matters worse, the cargo door locked in the open position and for the rest of the flight his crew clung to whatever bolted-down object they could grab and refused to even attempt to catch the items that, piece by piece, slid out the open door. The captain estimated that he lost over one-quarter of his load. A bracketed note on the last page of the report stated that all of the captain's expletives were edited out, and that a more complete version existed, should such a reference be necessary.

"Are you certain you can't make it?" he asked as he stood in the door to her office.

"No. I have so much work." She smiled.

Foxbourne ran his fingers through his hair. "But how will he understand?"

"Don't worry. He will understand when you hand him the check."

"Don't *you* want to give him the check?"

"No, Mr. Foxbourne."

"Thomas."

She took a short breath. "It is your case . . . Thomas. You give him the check."

"But at that rate I could just mail it to him."

She smiled. "Maybe you should. It would be much more simple that way."

He shook his head and walked off. In the hall he saw his boss, Mr. Takeshita, approaching. Foxbourne nodded.

"Very thorough work, Foxbourne," Takeshita said. "Very thorough."

"Thank you, sir," Foxbourne replied, vaguely aware of a mounting sense of unease. Everything had gone so well, he told himself. He'd all but rescued his, as well as Kim's, career and had just garnered one of the rare compliments his superior doled out. He should feel victorious. He *was* victorious.

On the drive to Niigata he managed to work himself into high spirits. Once again he felt considerably relieved that this comical blemish had been purged from his track record. And why? Why had he succeeded? Because he didn't know when to quit. Don't give up, don't ever give up! Keep pushing, and pushing, until you reach your goal! He decided as a treat later he'd buy himself dinner and might actually take the plunge and try sushi. See what the craze was all about.

When he reached the fisherman's house, he hopped out of his car and strolled up to the door, check in hand. He knocked on the door. After a moment it opened. Fumiyama smiled, bowed, and stepped aside for Foxbourne to enter.

"No, no, thank you," Foxbourne said and handed the man the check.

Fumiyama smiled more broadly and bowed again. "*Domo arigato,*" he said.

Foxbourne attempted a bow. *"Domo arigato,"* he replied.

Fumiyama motioned for him to come inside.

"No, no," Foxbourne said. "Must get back to office." He mimed typing into a keypad. "Work," he said.

Fumiyama smiled. "Work."

"Work," Foxbourne repeated, excited by getting a response. "I must tell you about the horse." He mimed riding a horse. "Horse."

"Yes, horse."

Foxbourne, thrilled to be so ably communicating, continued to mime the tale, stepping through a rather involved dance of sorts as he acted out the parts of the Horse, the Plane, Mako Iko, and Igor the Drunk One. Fumiyama applauded once he'd finished.

"The horse," Foxbourne said once he'd gotten back to his feet, "that fell and crashed through your boat."

Fumiyama smiled and nodded.

"Your boat, your boat," Foxbourne repeated as he pointed out at the ocean.

"Yes, yes. My boat."

"Your boat. Yes!"

"'Yes. My boat."

Foxbourne stared at the man, confused. "So your horse inside . . . it didn't come from heaven. It fell out of an airplane. There is an explanation."

"I don't need explanation. I have answer."

"You can't have an answer without an explanation. There's no equation. There's no . . . no . . ." Foxbourne stopped himself and stared at the fisherman. "You speak English," he said.

"Not good. That's why I speak Japanese to your friend. Very nice lady."

Foxbourne grimaced, remembering his pantomime. He took a step back, gathered himself. "Thank you very much, Mr. Fumiyama," he said. "I'm glad that Lloyd's of London at Tokyo was able to serve you, and I hope you'll consider us in the future for all your insurance needs."

That night Foxbourne sat in his tiny high-rise apartment and stared out the window at the building across from his, considering what his present rent would get him in Chicago, Boston, New York. He sketched on a notebook in his lap, trying to figure exactly how much longer he needed to stay in his position before he requested a transfer. He congratulated himself on solving the case. There was nothing but good to come out of it, he told himself. You're on your way, Foxbourne.

A few miles north of Niigata, Takashi Fumiyama placed his daily offering of a handful of hay and a cup of sake upon his altar to comfort the creature that had found itself swept up, then falling wingless through the sky. He sipped at his own cup and asked the spirit of the horse to comfort the American who had brought him his check that day, to maybe lead him to a calling that would serve him more fully. One using his body, Fumiyama felt certain. Perhaps a form of dance.

Steve Adams has had stories appear in *Glimmer Train* and elsewhere.

"I was hoping this section was about dating."

CROSSING BORDERS / *Adrie Kusserow*

Fiji—*Yalo* Spirits

In Fiji, *yalo* spirits
leave the body
to tattle on the self,
slippery essences closer to fog
than semen slide into the neighbors'
ears all the juicy details
of a married man's affairs.

What is kept inside the skull
grows like a tumor,
some smell it like a fetid
egg, sense it through an itching
breast, a vague sense of heat.

A woman's secret pregnancy
keeps a whole village from catching
fish, collapses a tune,
nudges the sick
closer to death.
Hair falls out,
cakes won't rise,
breasts dry up like prunes.

At night *niju* spirits
enter the body
through fluid contours of a dream.
Some possess the victim for days, as a dry voice,
illness or heaviness in the limbs,
the whole village crowding inside,
the young ones creeping through the windows
like monkeys, the elders hedging bets
on what it will take for the *niju*
to leave. The chief, too busy
bargaining with the *niju*,

designates two men
to urinate
for him.

April, New York—Anorexia Nervosa

In New York, a young girl lies alone
in her room, her bones
light as kindling, her mind heavy
as soggy fruit.
Too weak to rise,
she floats in a haze of lightheadedness.
What anchors her to the bed
is the small iron
box of will inside her,
her mind sliding over it, habitually,
like a tongue runs over the filling
of an old cavity.

At night she lies awake,
her fingers
tracing the terrain of her skin,
her Yale T-shirt absorbing
the night sweats
of a body locked in.

Outside, earth nudges its grubby paws
up through snow,
she smells hunger, gears shifting,
death grinding back into life.

She obsesses on the irony of bodies—
98 percent water, condemned to the life of a solid,
the way spring
makes the flesh
a cage.

Didn't she read, in Mungara, the dead are soaked
in oils and salt,
the skin falling off the bones
like wet leaves from a limb?
The soul resides

in what drips to the cup, the rest
discarded for scrap.

She figures she still looks pretty normal,
thin, yes, but no one back at the dorm has spoken to her.
She hears her mother creep up the stairs,
knock gently, asking politely
would she like to talk. No thank you,
she hears leaving her mouth, a strange voice
made of gossamer fabric from a country
she has never seen.

Her mother's shadow
slithers under the doorway
over her bones like a stream over rocks.
She dares not enter,
obeying as she must the gods
of privacy
lodged like gargoyles
outside her door.
She wants to say,
Mama, wait,
to lie with her
like bark
in the rich dark light.

What saves her
is the steel box of will
inside her—
its gravitational pull,
its cultural charisma.
How easily it reels her frail body back,
branding her with an *I*.

HUNTING DOWN THE MONK/
Adrie Kusserow

After my father's death, I knocked
on my mother's door,
me four feet tall, red leather purse in hand,
fingers soft as bread
and told her I am headed to a nunnery.
I was going to God
and there was nothing she could do
but take the small nun
in my size 6 habit (headdress lifted from the armchair
    cover)
against the slack
of her belly
and contain me for the night.

Even then I knew a good high
when I felt it,
the buzz of grabbing the tail end
of some god's magnetic pull, like a baby
finally latching on to the nipple for a good hard drag.
That day I was taken from school
I rode to the hospital
in the back of Mrs. Farmer's Chevy
saving my saliva in a Twinkie bag stolen
from a mean girl's lunch,
she thinking I was throwing up
from the shock,
me wanting to bathe his skull
in what I knew
was good and warm.

Nineteen, wandering in the Himalayas, at a monastery
in the clouds, I had just drunk the water
from a stream, hoping to get sick, sitting
at the feet of a monk
whose skin I had groped the night before,

hating myself, didn't I know better,
looking for God in the places
our bodies fed on each
other, instead of the space between.
Despite the teachings, the endless sitting, he was agitated,
    fumbling
inside his own locked house, setting it back in order.

And he did,
and I was lonely again,
thinking of my father, my first love,
my first household god, skull smashed
like a watermelon, the seeds lying
on the highway like small fish out of water.

How come we aren't told there are no gods, and how
    come we still look,
knowing they surface
because we feed them.
Shouldn't there be a name for us,
the nomads who wander
from meaning station to station,
the ones who know better,
the ones who get hooked.

ORPHANAGE, MISSIONARIES OF CHARITY, KATHMANDU, NEPAL/
Adrie Kusserow

Praise ugliness.
Praise selfishness, greed.

Praise all that protrudes—
the last red flags
of the living.

Praise this little shop of horrors,
the children who reach
me first, ferociously claiming
one limb
as their own.

Praise those who squirm
onto my lap
squeezing between others,
soaking on the banks of skin
like lizards in the sun.

Praise those crouched
on tables, grooming each other like apes.

Praise the greedy suck and slurp of gruel
from thirty tin plates.

Praise the rocky spine of the five-year-old,
shoulder blades poked up like a bat,
crouching on her perch
mute, gray, watchful as a gargoyle.

Praise the girl no one will touch,
her body a patchwork of scabies.
Praise the sisters who swim out
to her island with naked hands

to smear her limbs
with heavy cream.

Praise for the boy with worms,
his belly red and bloated as a Madagascar frog's
puffing itself in the heat
of courtship.

Praise the one they call *crazed witch*
for prowess with her claws,
darting from bunk bed to bed
scratching the eyes of the sleeping.
Praise the way she flies
onto your back, biting your neck,
her face blossoming with rage.

Praise the scrappy ones with necks of string,
the girl I thought was a boy—
her gender humbly excusing itself
in favor of bone.
the slack skin of her rear
wrinkled like dried fruit,

Praise the tiniest ones sitting in a row
on plastic potties,
spines curved and soft as shrimp,
heads heavy as watermelons.
Praise them crapping yellow ribbons
of rice and curry,
falling from the toilets
like Humpty Dumpty over the great wall.

Praise those dangling
over the balcony
onto the streets of Kathmandu—
squealing
as we pry them from the edge.
How intently they focus!
that last moment, their sharp eyes feeding
on the lives of the living
before they are brought back in.

BULIMIA RELIGIOSA / *Adrie Kusserow*

I'm dainty, I never eat in public.

On the surface
I say a delicate no-thank-you
to the Jehovah's Witnesses
who crawl like ants
around this town
bringing goodies to the door—
the warm pamphlet
with its simple ingredients
only God's words,
the whole truth, no additives
or preservatives.

To the Unitarian Universalists
with their low-cal we're not this or that,
which only leads to harsher
cravings for the real thing
(Greek Orthodox incense,
sacrificing a big cow),
I say no.

At night I lie in bed,
anemic, sick of prison gruel and diet-meaning,
thinking of those cheap, creamy answers.
I start to salivate,
I sneak downstairs,
I say fuck it,
I inhale their fat truths,
soft pamphlets and colorful creeds,
I cram two, sometimes
three, images of happy multicultural people
(hanging peacefully with death)
into my mouth till I can
barely breathe, Armageddon's sugar
dripping down my chin.

Stuffed
I hippo up the stairs,
crawl into bed bloated,
the blood leaving my brain
for finer pastures down below,
numb for the first time in months,
the thoughts happily nibbling
like moths on Jehovah's
latest issue of *Watch Tower.*

CONFESSION / *Adrie Kusserow*

I come from a tribe of women
ruled by a God, lean and tall,
long, stern face of white stone.
Principles He laid out
like a formal table.

My sisters and I
were born
on His white linen tablecloth
our swollen pink bodies
all covered with smut and paste,
our liquids soaking into the table.
What He hated most
was when He touched us—
we leaked like toads.

At sixteen, we tiptoed around Him,
felt fat and smelly as shrimp, our silly breasts
sometimes escaping our corsets,
swinging like bombs
into His teacups.

We worried He could smell us
like the compost pile out back,
so on Sundays, we bathed, dried our fetid
crotches, the clean cotton underwear lying like
brides on the chair. Locked in now, safe,
we marched to church, the unclosed parts of us
fresh as pieces of fruit in a Ziploc bag.

Still, my sisters and I
worshipped that Man, loving and fearing
the red-wine smell
of Him leaning close,
so close
His breath scorched us,

the longest of his eyebrow hairs
pricking us like the legs
of white spiders.

Adrie Kusserow is a finalist in this year's Larry Levis Editors' Prize Contest.

"Sorry. I must have dozed off
while you were complaining."

RACE THOUGHTS/*Carl Schiffman*

"IT'S BAD ENOUGH I'm a nigger, but I've got to be ugly, too!" Words overheard a few months ago on a Canarsie-bound L train in the New York City subway: the speaker a teenaged black girl, talking to three or four friends on their way home from school. The other girls laughed, as she did; her tone was not bitter or angry but communicated a rueful good humour, as though she were acknowledging a joke that life had played at her expense.

How had we come full circle, to the most deprecatory word anyone, including a black, could use to describe a dark-skinned person of African origin—a word that, more than any other, echoes the experience of slavery? I, a white person, had spent over twenty-five years working for black equality, first as a state and federal civil rights investigator and then as a writer and fund-raiser for a wide range of nationally known black nonprofit organizations. Had I—and the hundreds or thousands of whites like me who had taken the civil rights struggle as our own, as America's most important unfinished domestic business— just been wasting our time? Even more unsettling to contemplate, had we been doing harm when we thought we were doing good?

I had grown up in an ethnically mixed neighborhood in Manhattan's upper West Side, had at least one Negro kid in all my classes right through high school, had known Negro and Puerto Rican kids who played ball on our primarily Jewish block after school. I had had a black roommate and a black close friend in college, and prior to working in civil rights, I had been a counselor in treatment centers for mentally disturbed or predelinquent adolescents in Dobbs Ferry, New York, and Hamden, Connecticut, where many of the kids in residence were black. I had also worked as a child welfare case worker, supervising the placement of state wards, many of them black, in Connecticut foster homes and treatment institutions. I thought, in other words, that I was pretty knowledgeable about the way Connecticut blacks lived.

What I discovered when I began work as a state civil rights investigator in Connecticut in 1968 was a society that was almost as segregated by custom as the South had been segregated by law. In the arms and armaments industries that were among Connecticut's principal employers, and in the other traditional industries that lined the Naugatuck Valley, black employees had been confined to jobs as jani-

---

tors or to the lowest and dirtiest occupations as unskilled laborers. Their lines of employment and seniority were kept separate from the lines of white employees, and the unions did nothing to bridge that separation. Just the contrary: office and sales jobs were all but hermetically sealed against blacks.

Employment discrimination was complemented by housing discrimination that was, if anything, more absolutely rigid. A New Haven suburb, East Haven, only five minutes away by car and ten by city bus from a large concentration of blacks, had zero black residents. School boundaries were drawn in conformity with racially frozen residential patterns so that virtually all-black or all-white "neighborhood" elementary schools were the rule. Most local police and fire departments, including the state police, were hostile to employing any blacks at all and threw up barrier after barrier against hiring them. Employment testing exploded into massive use just as equal employment legislation went into effect. I came to understand that despite the civil rights revolution in the South and the sympathy it won for Southern blacks fighting legal segregation, in the North most blacks, although the pejorative word was rarely used, were still thought of and treated as "niggers."

I also found a black community devastated by its experience of exclusion, hardly prepared to take advantage of the equality of treatment the new civil rights laws purported to guarantee. There were some blacks, frequently light-skinned and the scions of a black elite, who were ready to take immediate advantage of the opportunities opened by equal employment legislation. Some of them moved into government work to help enforce the new laws; others were snapped up by businesses with government contracts that needed to mollify investigators from the OFCC, the Office of Federal Contract Compliance, which was beginning to apply some noncoercive but annoying pressure. Still others, perhaps the least qualified of black college graduates, got jobs as "equal employment officers" in personnel departments where they specialized in dealing with other minority employees, were listed as "executives" and yet had no line authority over white employees. There was, in any case, an extreme minority of blacks who were capable of competing on equal terms with whites for employment. The lifting of external barriers, to the extent that they were really lifted, did not make blacks, who had been excluded from such competition for generations, ready to compete.

A few unhappy experiences have stayed in my mind from those early days of civil rights enforcement. A young black couple was told that a house in a small town north of New Haven had already been rented. White friends of theirs called and were told the property was still available. The enforcement machinery worked perfectly: an injunction was issued within a couple of days, a court hearing was held within two weeks and the landlord was ordered to rent to the couple. Within six months, though, the couple had broken up, the man had moved away, and the woman was eventually evicted for nonpayment of rent.

A night watchman position in a warehouse was not given to a black applicant with previous guard experience. To settle the complaint, the employer agreed to hire him; within a month there was a spate of unauthorized absences and a couple of alleged instances, not contested by the employee, of his coming to work drunk. When he was discharged, another black was hired, and he, too, turned out to be unreliable and alcoholic. I don't recall whether the employer was constrained to try a third time.

Much more bleakly revelatory than these isolated instances was a meeting I held, at one of their homes on a Sunday evening, with a group of seven or eight black employees of a Naugatuck Valley manufacturing firm. They had all worked for twenty years or more on an assembly line, producing a variety of mechanical home products that white salesmen sold and serviced. The whites were actually trained by the blacks to do the repairs. When a black asked about possible promotion to salesman, he was brushed off, threatened with discharge if he persisted in his request. The sales jobs were cleaner and paid much better, but the blacks were concerned that if they filed a complaint, they would lose the jobs they already had. These were middle-aged men who had built their lives around these segregated jobs. They owned their own homes, had nice furniture and cars, some had children in college. They had adjusted to second-class citizenship and were not prepared to risk what they had on the strength of a new law whose provisions against retaliation had not yet been adequately tested in the courts. They were so afraid that their employer would discover they had even talked to a civil rights worker that they had insisted on the Sunday meeting and on my using my personal car rather than my assigned state vehicle. I was too unsure myself to pressure them to take any action. The complaints were never filed, and as far as I know the men remained on the assembly line until they retired.

Many major employers, under both legal and moral pressure, and usually against the bitter opposition of whatever labor unions were involved, made legitimate efforts to open up their work force, including professional and managerial positions, to blacks. What happened all too frequently was that the policy of equal employment ran headlong into the unpreparedness of large segments of the black labor force.

Black production workers were late or absent more frequently than their white counterparts; they were less efficient; they did not take orders well. Black office workers were deficient in spelling or simple arithmetic; did not understand or adapt well to routine office procedures.

The bulk of the complaints I dealt with in Connecticut and then a couple of years later, when I transferred to the more powerful federal Equal Employment Opportunity Commission (EEOC), came not from job applicants but from present employees alleging discrimination in disciplinary action or promotion. And it was certainly true that in companies that had hired reluctantly or where lower-level supervisors were hostile to integration, blacks were dismissed for lateness or attendance problems when whites with the same bad records were retained. Blacks were discharged or penalized for "insubordination" where white employees who had behaved the same way were let off with a warning. Blacks were denied promotions for reasons that were not found applicable to white candidates.

One consequence of white employers' overreaction is that it allowed underperforming blacks to brush aside even legitimate criticism of their behavior by calling it "racist."

I have sometimes wondered whether the initial staffing of the EEOC, a new agency created to enforce Title VII of the 1964 Civil Rights Act, was a case of good intentions gone awry or a cynical ploy to undermine enforcement. The staff on all levels except that of attorney was predominantly minority, far from young, and drawn from other federal agencies. New hires were also predominantly minority. For the full period of my employment there I was the highest-ranking nonattorney white in the New York region.

The Connecticut Commission had been cobbled together with state employees from other agencies, too, but the director there, Arthur L. Green, a black, showed no hesitancy in transferring back or discharging the white deadwood he had been sent. Nor did he hesitate to discharge nonperforming blacks. And his new hires tended to be young and committed. The EEOC, by contrast, seemed to have no standards of performance for its own minority employees. In the view of the EEOC, minority underperformance did not, could not, exist. White supervisors, one of whom had been physically assaulted by a black employee shortly before I started there, were afraid to take disciplinary action for fear of being called racist and seeing their careers destroyed; black supervisors protected even the most unproductive of other blacks.

A few examples of what I found should be more than enough to illustrate the problems. The New York office, which handled all of New England as well, had no system for assigning cases. There were no priorities. Complaints could not even be investigated in chronological order because there was no filing system for new cases, just a row of cabinets into which files were shoved at random. Supervisors would simply go to file cabinets, take out an armful of case files, and distribute them a few at a time to the investigators. Cases that affected thousands of employees and might have had national significance languished in the files, while absurd or petty complaints (to cite the most extreme example, the case of an employee who accused her employer of "hexing" her were assigned for investigation. It took me months, once I had become a supervisor myself, to get the files in reasonable order and to establish priorities for at least the cases I supervised.

Right from its inception, one of the major complaints about the EEOC, both from the minority community and from white civil rights activists, was the incredible delay in investigating complaints and the enormous backlog of uninvestigated cases that kept growing and growing. The EEOC did set production standards for its investigators, but when two black probationary investigators failed to complete two cases each in six months, falling lamentably short of agency standards and without any indication that they would ever do much better, I was called a "racist" for suggesting they be returned to their former federal jobs, and a black supervisor found a way of doctoring their records so they became permanent employees. So many investigators proved unable to write up investigations in an acceptable way that a relatively junior white investigator was assigned to do the writing, and since the investigations were frequently incomplete because of inadequate supervision, he also took responsibility for telling the investigators what additional information they needed to get.

Even worse, to my mind—far more discouraging than the inability of many blacks at EEOC to do their assigned jobs in a minimally acceptable way—was the extraordinary indifference most of my black fellow employees showed to the complaints and complainants the agency dealt with. There was no commitment, no sense of urgency, no appreciation of the revolution that could be accomplished if the agency worked well. There was more talk about barbecue grills and automatic garage doors—middle-class suburban acquisitions—than about civil rights. One of the investigators referred to complainants with annoyance, calling them "those people." Had she been white, she could have been called racist. Or maybe what she was most concerned about was social class. "Those people," who worked with their hands, were not her people. She used to send thank-you notes to companies she investigated for the coffee or snacks they gave her during the course of her on-site visits, as though they had been social calls.

A number of the investigations I conducted or supervised resulted in cases filed in federal court by private attorneys or nonprofit law firms. There were positive consequences of any well-conducted investigation, too, in advance of any court action. The company being investigated would want to limit its liability, would make changes to conform to the law now, whatever its behavior might have been in the past. The job was not without real satisfactions, but toward the end, the only way I survived was by assigning myself cases as far from our office as possible: paper mills in New Hampshire—fly to Portland, drive the Presidentials; military contractors in Massachusetts—fly to Springfield, drive the Berkshires. Beautiful scenery to balance the permanent bad taste in my mouth.

My only activity at the EEOC that prompted legal action by the agency itself was a sex-discrimination case my wife filed and I shepherded through the agency appeal process. It resulted in establishing an important principle about the illegality of gender "preferences" and caused the New York State Employment Service to stop using different-colored application forms: blue for male, "salmon" for female job applicants.

All the black and civil rights organizations I worked for—generally via a profit-making consulting firm—after I left the EEOC relied heavily on financial support from the white community. My job was to help raise money from that community. I think most whites believed, as I did, that support for these organizations would bring us closer to the realization of two goals: firstly, an end to traditional white racism as it affected all aspects of black life; secondly, the provision of remedial and supportive services, especially educational services, to the black community to enable it to fully participate in the life of the larger society once the artificial barriers of discrimination had been removed. In other words, the hope was to address both sides of the double bind of white racism and black underperformance, to bring blacks up to speed while brushing racist whites out of their way.

Most whites, and possibly even many blacks, would probably agree that the defeat of traditional white racism has been largely achieved. There is no major aspect of American life in 1999—housing employment, education, public accommodations, voting rights—in which discrimination against blacks is not illegal. There are still violent attacks on blacks by vicious whites, but the law goes after these whites—even when the vicious attackers are policemen—as it never did during the first three centuries of black habitation on these shores.

Black underperformance, though, especially academic underperformance—to which other social woes are crucially linked—has shown remarkable tenacity. It has been both announced and demonstrated to the black community that college scholarships and the prospects of good jobs afterward, entree into the American middle class or beyond, are available to blacks who do even moderately well in high school, not just to the academic stars. Black college students know that graduate schools will compete to enroll the top tier of black college graduates, but despite all the active encouragement that has supplanted discrimination, blacks continue to do poorly on both high school and college achievement tests. Even in the lower grades, the results can be disheartening. Why should this be the case when white racism has largely transformed itself, however temporarily or grudgingly, into white benevolence? And when tens of millions of white charitable dollars have gone to support black educational institutions?

There are a number of identifiably black colleges in the United States, mostly in the South. They fall into two major groups, not counting Howard University, which is a special case. One group, the United Negro College Fund (UNCF) schools, consists of private institutions, many of them started by Northern church groups during Reconstruction, to provide educational opportunity to the newly freed slaves. There are around forty of these schools, some of the better known of which are Booker T. Washington's Tuskegee Institute, Morehouse, Fisk, and Spelman. These schools have always been open to white students and faculty and have never, to my knowledge, been subject to any kind of desegregation order.

The other group consists of approximately forty state colleges in nineteen states, including Delaware, West Virginia, Ohio and Pennsylvania, that were the separate and unequal black portions of segregated state systems of higher education. These systems were ordered to desegregate by the Supreme Court over thirty years ago; the case that covers them, and has lasted about as long as *Jarndyce v. Jarndyce* in Dickens' *Bleak House*, is now called *United States v. Fordice* and has created terrible problems for the black civil rights community, especially for its leading law firm, the NAACP Legal Defense Fund (LDF).

The principle that allowed the LDF to win *Brown v. Board of Education*—that separate is inherently unequal—applied exactly to these state schools. In terms of faculty training, physical facilities, and educational outcomes, these identifiably black schools lagged atrociously behind their white counterparts. Black civil rights agencies sued to have the systems merged, only to discover tremendous resistance on the part of the black population, not just current students or faculty but whole communities for whom these segregated colleges had been major cultural institutions. These schools had deep roots in the black community, had traditions—marching bands, football teams, fraternities and sororities, the whole college panoply, all of which might be swallowed up and destroyed by the stronger white schools if the systems were to be merged. What jobs would there be then for black faculty and administrators? Wouldn't they just be pensioned off, their useful lives cut short?

The civil rights organizations backed away from *U.S. v. Fordice,* and these schools, still overwhelmingly black, still academically inferior, supply seventy-five percent of all college degrees earned by blacks in public colleges in the United States. The UNCF schools, a goodly number of them anyway, are academically weaker than the black state colleges, and even the best of them are being preserved not because of their academic strength but because they are black institutions and have histories inseparable from the black experience in America. I am talking about the institutions through which a group defines its own identity. What their graduates do on LSATs or GREs may be a relatively minor matter.

Many blacks who have emerged from the ghetto into successful professional life, many teachers in inner-city schools, many forthright black community leaders, will acknowledge that a black kid who does well in school, who studies hard, may be subject to scorn and harrassment, possibly even to physical abuse at the hands of his schoolmates for "acting like whitey." Is this sort of behavior simply sour grapes on the part of youngsters who know they are going to fail and don't want to be shown up by a classmate's success? Or does it cut much deeper than that, have resonance with Southern blacks' support for their traditional schools, roots in a genuine desire to preserve black identity? And what might that identity be?

The American black community is extraordinarily diverse. It has important currents flowing from the Spanish- or French-speaking Caribbean as well as from former English colonies such as Jamaica or Barbados. Different parts of the North received migratory flows from different regions of the South in two separate major waves coinciding with or immediately following the two World Wars. Differences of skin tone, reflecting the sexual predations of white planters and carrying forward the "privileges" of a "café au lait" mulatto class, still play a complex role, putting black identity under great strain from within.

The methods used by sociologists or census takers, or test evaluators, for that matter, are completely inadequate to describe or quantify the complexities of black experience. What most unites this community is the shared history of slavery and segregation, of abuse and humiliation, of being treated as moral and intellectual inferiors, objects of fear and contempt, second- or third-class citizens, by whites who have acted as if dominance were their birthright. To what extent is "acting like whitey" an acceptance of that dominance, a betrayal of black identity?

Slavery denied black men the right to support and raise their own children. And still, today, in the ghettos, black men in great number, because they are unemployed or addicted or in jail, do not take responsibility for their own children. Black women were not allowed, as slaves, sexual modesty and control of their own bodies. And still, today, in the ghettos, multiple fathers for multiple children and widespread promiscuity are commonplace. Blacks in slavery and for generations afterward were kept illiterate or nearly so. And still, today, in the ghettos, learning to read well, to study hard, is "acting like whitey."

Identity forged by oppressors is still identity. The lives that those black assembly-line workers in the Naugatuck Valley built for themselves as second-class citizens were real lives, with values to be defended and preserved. Even the black supervisors at the EEOC who chose to retain less-than-competent trainees may have been affirming a personal solidarity among blacks that was far more meaningful to them than conformity to job standards imposed on them by a white bureaucracy.

The last several years have seen a tendency in many black communities to use political power to undo *Brown v. Board. of Education* even at the grade school level. Blacks will do a better job of insisting on high standards for their own children, this view asserts, than will whites, many of whom will simply let black students drift because they do not believe blacks are intelligent enough to learn. A black teacher who insists on high standards for his pupils, who criticizes their shortcomings, can hardly be called a racist, although he or she will may have to get past accusations of "acting white."

If the historically black colleges were dependent for survival on the gifts of their own alumni rather than on state and federal subsidies or white charitable contributions, they would have to provide their students with a competitive education. As things stand—with white money pouring in from outside—these black schools maintain both low academic standards and the nation's highest rate of student loan default.

There is a substantial black middle class out there, the product of the last thirty years of civil rights activity, that has to decide whether it wants to invest its money and skills in making black institutions—not just the traditionally black colleges but also the NAACP and the Urban League and the Legal Defense Fund and a host of other presently white-funded organizations—both truly autonomous and not second-rate. There is nothing autonomous about black studies departments in white-financed universities. White funders, corporations, foundations, government agencies, and, I suspect, even universities, are exceptionally soft on black-led organizations, demand little in the way of performance, not even financial accountability, and are afraid perhaps, and not without reason, of being called "racist" if they ask too much.

In terms of autonomy, the most successful black institutions that exist today are the membership-funded professional organizations of black engineers or computer programmers or businessmen, or even of black policemen and firemen protecting their interests in bigoted urban departments.

Above all, and most successful to my mind, is one of the very few black national organizations that does not have deep roots in slavery or segregation, that rejects second-class citizenship and that scorns white help. I certainly count on making no new friends among its membership, but I'm sure that if that girl on the subway or her family had belonged to the Nation of Islam, she would never even have dreamed of calling herself a "nigger."

Carl Schiffman, a finalist in this year's Editors' Prize Contest, has published work in numerous literary magazines, including a previous appearance in *The Missouri Review*.

THE SPRING HOUSE/*William Richardson*

Both Abraham and Sarah had grown very old, and Sarah was past the age of childbearing. So Sarah laughed to herself and said, "I am past bearing children now that I am old and out of my time, and my husband is old." The Lord said to Abraham, "Why did Sarah laugh and say, 'Shall I indeed bear a child when I am old?' Is anything impossible for the Lord? In due season I shall come back to you, about this time next year, and Sarah shall have a son." Sarah lied because she was frightened, and denied that she had laughed; but He said, "Yes, you did laugh."

Genesis 18:11–15

I BUY BREAD FROM JAKE Smucker every Friday at Gratz Crossroads. There is nothing remarkable about this farmers' market where the Amish from the surrounding District Churches come to sell; it could be any one of many scattered throughout the abundant central Pennsylvania farmlands. But there, three years ago, in the midst of produce stalls and butchers' cases, I saw an old Amish man and his wife selling bread—the bread Jake now bakes—and I was so struck by their appearance that I approached their stall, wanting grace.

It happened to me once, in Notre Dame de Paris, at the communion rail. Following the elevation of the host, the priest put the wafer on my tongue and said, "Corps du Christ." I looked into an old cleric's eyes and received grace. It has not happened since, and when I tried to make it happen—to see grace in a simple loaf of bread—I thought I had found it, but it was only my imaginings.

I suppose my mistake was believing I could make it happen, thinking grace was something I could take as easily as buying a loaf of bread. I imagined it simple, like a wafer on the tongue. But the loaf was no sacrament. It did not change, although I insisted on its elevation and tried to make it something holy. When I ceased to look for the mysteries I imagined hidden in the loaf, I saw instead its makers' plainness: two simple Amish women and two half-brothers with the same bright blue eyes. If there is grace, it is in Jake's and Isaac's eyes, not in Emma's determined face or Suzie's arresting smile, and it was never in the bread.

Isaac and Suzie Smucker, who first baked the bread, appeared as beatific and perfect in their earthly goodness as if they had stepped off the face of a holy card. But if goodness radiated from them, protected them, as prayers tell us goodness protects the saints, why did their house burn down, and why did they move away? After the fire, Isaac sold the bread business to his younger half-brother, Jake, a mason with more work than he can do. Why he wants to get up at 2:00 A.M. to mix and bake bread I can't imagine, unless it's to keep the business in the family, the Community. But that's the way it is. Now Jake and Emma bake the bread.

Isaac and Suzie Smucker moved back to Lancaster County. Now that they are gone, no one in their Amish community speaks of them. It is as if they never lived here, never existed. Their position is inferior to those who have simply died, and although Isaac and Suzie are not dead, I must speak about them in the past tense.

Last winter I spent the short hours of February afternoons with Isaac in his workshop, where he taught me how to plane boards smoothly by exhaling with the drag of the plane, as in a meditation. He was a small man, in his early seventies, with the slight build of those Pennsylvania Amish who have intermarried for generations. His hands were the competent, careful hands of a master craftsman who has made furniture all his life for the young Amish girls who marry each year in the flurry of November weddings. Isaac made beds and dressers, deal tables, sometimes a corner cupboard, but mainly chests, those standard storage pieces of all Pennsylvania households, both plain and fancy. He worked his cabinetry in white oak, a wood without pretense that lends itself to simple, functional designs. He worked in a watchful silence, but his blue eyes spoke to the wood as he patiently matched and planed the smooth white boards. Whether speckled with sawdust from his carpentry or with flour from kneading the loaves that Suzie baked, Isaac's face had an indefatigable, often mischievous, cheerfulness. When the wood shavings in his beard caught the light of the late winter sun, he looked like a sculpture in progress—an august icon of Amish hard work.

Suzie was a few years younger than her husband. With her elegant carriage, delicate, rounded cheekbones, and perfect teeth—so white they looked false but were not—she was striking. But when I try to remember Suzie, to fix her image in my mind from those times I saw her selling bread or bringing us refreshments in Isaac's workshop, all I see is her smile. I could not tell you the color of her eyes. Her smile was so forthright, so guileless, that it pulled me into it, away from her eyes and seemingly further. It hypnotized me. Suzie's smile proclaimed, "Look! This is all there is and all there should be; there is nothing more." It was both startling and mysterious, a smile I have not seen in art—"images of the World," as the Amish say. I have never seen God, but I imagined that Suzie's smile reflected the grace of someone who had, it was so radiant.

Suzie's smile both captivated and disturbed me because I saw ecstasy in it. Face to face, I never thought it false. But since Jake told me why she and Isaac went back to Lancaster County, I have asked myself, Was it artifice—a mask to hide what it was not?

I have only seen Emma twice. I first saw her at the market, after she became baker of the bread. She is a small, fine-boned woman in her forties, some years younger than her sister-in-law, with only a touch of gray in her hair. Emma's delicate features would make her beautiful if not for her knitted forehead, the visible tension at her mouth. Emma looked tired and careworn that raw May day as she pulled her insubstantial shawl tight against the wind and hurried inside to escape the cold. Her face told no Good News, professed no acceptance of her earthly lot, unlike the animated face of her sister-in-law with its startling smile. As she hurried past, I wondered whether, for Emma, baking was simply another chore in a life of chores that she performed without comment, unlike her sister-in-law, whose work seemed to be a form of prayer. But Emma's bread is just as good.

Buying bread from Isaac, with his indefatigable cheerfulness, and from Suzie, with her arresting smile, became something more than simple necessity. In my imagination, I transformed the Smuckers into the saints I wanted them to be, and in their presence, I experienced the feelings some report when confronted with personalities like Mother Teresa. They had a charisma I had never encountered. Their presence affected me with feelings of unworthiness, even self-doubt, and by simply buying a loaf of their bread, I felt elevated.

Once during my preoccupation with the Smuckers, I saw Isaac and Suzie at a farm sale and I spent the day watching them instead of the auctioneer. Farm auctions in central Pennsylvania are held outside, on the lawns of the farmhouses. The auctioneer's helpers pass the goods through the open windows, move them out, line them up, get them ready for the next bidding. At these auctions people bring folding chairs and form an expectant audience seated in a semicircle, their attention commanded by the auctioneer and his goods. Isaac and Suzie had only one chair between them, and Isaac sat while Suzie stood patiently behind, her hands resting on her husband's shoulders. I offered Suzie my chair, but she declined to take it and stood throughout the auction.

All morning the young Amish men who wanted to purchase the farm or its equipment came to Isaac for his advice as an elder of their Community. From a distance, I saw a *tableau vivant* of righteousness, and I tried to name the source of their grace, to take in their goodness, to believe as I had once believed in the worn holy pictures in my child's missal.

In my obsession—a staring I felt drawn into—I tried to penetrate their aura, but I could not. Some days later I asked Mima, the unmarried Amish girl who comes to clean my house, about Isaac and Suzie. Although they were in her District Church and one of Mima's sisters had married a Smucker, she did not know them well; they had moved only recently from Lancaster County. What Mima did say was that Suzie and Isaac were unusual in their Amish Community because they were childless. Among the Amish, Mima remarked, children are seen as a blessing from God and large families are common. Some childless couples she knew took in foster children—even cared for AIDS babies from Philadelphia—but the Smuckers had not.

When Amish District Church holy days fell on Fridays, Suzie and Isaac did not come to market. I missed my bread if I neglected to buy ahead, and I always forgot Ascension Day—when Jesus Christ left the earth and went up into heaven to be with his Father. Although not as widely celebrated in Pennsylvania as in Europe, Ascension Day is, for the devout, still a holiday of closed businesses. Old-fashioned Lutheran families picnic in the woods, and the Amish go fishing. The day of the fire was Ascension Day, so I didn't know something had happened until the next week.

"The Smuckers lost everything—absolutely everything!" Mima reported about the Ascension Day fire when she came to clean the following Monday. Through Mima I gave what she and I thought the Smuckers could accept: money, sheets, and towels. Because I am not Amish, I was indirect about my small gift; Mima took it to the elders of the District Church. Then—it was the same week as the fire—Isaac and Suzie Smucker disappeared.

"They're gone," Mima said, fixing her eyes on her soup when I asked about the Smuckers at lunch the next Monday. She was obviously uncomfortable talking about them. I though it strange, but I didn't pursue it. A week later Mima reported that the District Church had rebuilt the burned house. I asked why, since the Smuckers had left.

"A house belongs to the Community," she explained. "When one is lost, we replace it. Another member of the Community will move into the house."

I didn't ask, and Mima didn't volunteer, who that might be.

As I bought strawberries that Friday at the stand that Mr. Steele, my Mennonite neighbor, tends at market, I overheard fragments of gossip in Pennsylvania-German dialect: ". . . drying apples on the stove, and the schnitz rack got hot, caught fire," someone said; ". . . not away, not visiting his father in Lancaster County at the time of the fire," Mr. Steele remarked. Why had he left the Lancaster County farm where he had lived all his life, moved north, built a new house? a woman asked. "He had another fire in Lancaster County," Mr. Steele said.

I carefully inspected Mr. Steele's crates of strawberries for as long as I could without attracting attention, but no one mentioned Suzie. Was that the role of Amish women: in the background, outside comment?

Monday morning, Mr. Steele pulled into my driveway and made me a gift of a second crate of strawberries—his wife had no more room in her freezer. He told me what he had learned about the Smuckers.

"When I offered to help the District Church rebuild the burned house, they said my help wasn't needed," Mr. Steele reported, still stung by the rebuff. "All the District Church did was buy the Smuckers a new set of aluminum cookware!" Mr. Steele, who never speaks ill of anyone, added, "A gift like that is mean—out of proportion to their tragedy. My Amish neighbors on the next dairy farm down the valley won't even talk about the Smuckers. All they said was that Isaac's half-brother, Jake, would take over the bread business. Jake's a mason. What does he know about baking bread?" Mr. Steele asked of no one in particular. "But," he concluded, throwing up his hands and climbing back into his truck, "who can understand the Amish?"

Mima, who is always friendly with Mr. Steele, was inside cleaning, but she never came out of the house.

I first saw Jake after he took over the bakery business at market. I asked after Isaac and Suzie: Were they all right? Did they need any- thing? The Smuckers were gone, and I missed them. Like Mr. Steele, I, too, wanted to know the reason. When I asked, Jake replied, "Those things happen," with a shortness implying that I should not have asked. Jake did not offer to introduce himself, and this made our acquaintance seem strangely anonymous. The next two Fridays, when I came to buy bread, Jake Smucker greeted me with, "Where do you live?" and I replied, "In the big house in Greenbrier, over in the next valley." So we began to watch each other.

I saw Jake at a farm sale. By then I knew, through Mima, that he was aware that the English man had made a donation to Isaac and Suzie. Yet all that day, Jake and I never spoke Isaac's or Suzie's or each other's names. He acknowledged me perfunctorily, but when our eyes met, he conveyed what seemed a different greeting—a cryptic protocol. It was a raw May day, and a painful spring damp penetrated my clothing. I huddled in a doorway to protect myself from the wind. As I watched

Jake talk with other Amish, I realized that his District Church members wore thin polyester year-round. I was miserable from the raw cold but determined to stay to buy a splint basket I spied at the bottom of a pile. I also stayed to spy on Jake.

I didn't imagine it: Jake watched me throughout the sale. Why? To see to whom I spoke? To see if I knew silence? If I understood the degrees of silence practiced by the descendants of the German population of central Pennsylvania? The Lutheran and Reformed are highly sociable, ever ready for news and gossip. The Mennonites stand apart from this jolly fellowship. While they generally abstain from spreading news, they participate as eager listeners. The Amish, in the world but not of the world, exist in a nonspeculative reality of things as they are. They do not indulge in gossip and turn from it in silence when it presents itself. They do not testify in court or bear witness against their neighbors, and when they shun a member of their Community as a sanction against disobedience, they do not speak to or of that person.

That afternoon, Jake approached me and said he wanted to buy the electric stove to use in his bread-baking business. He explained that his District Church allowed the use of electricity outside the house. The bread business was now located in his barn. He asked my opinion about the ancient stove at the sale that stood in the corner of the hot farm kitchen where everyone had crowded to avoid the harsh wind. I told Jake it was too old—he would not be able to get parts—and offered to sell him, for a dollar, a newer stove I had stored in my attic since I had redecorated my kitchen and switched to gas. He accepted.

On Monday, Mima's cleaning day, when I took her home, I stopped at Jake's to deliver his "electric range." After we put it in the barn, Jake walked me back to my truck, which was parked in front of his house. I saw Jake's family, or at least part of it. On the porch were teenaged girls I had noticed helping him at market and a brood of little blond boys, the younger two identical twins. From inside, Emma appeared, issued a stern order in dialect, and the children dispersed and disappeared. A younger woman came out on the porch of the old house across the creek. "That's my married daughter," Jake remarked. She was as curious to see me as I was to see her. Slowly and deliberately, she shook her rugs, hung them to air on the porch railing and watched all the while I spoke to her father. It seemed that Jake and Emma had three families—three sets of children spread over some thirty years.

"What can I do to help you out?" Jake asked as I was leaving—his way of thanking me for the burners.

"Would you have a look at the mortar on my spring house before haying season?" I asked.

"I can do that," Jake said. "That's what I do: fix things."

This summer is fine weather for haying. Rain alternates with stretches of hot, dry days, and a second crop of hay comes immediately after the first cutting. Jake calls from his phone in the barn—there's none in the house—to say that he cannot come when we had agreed because there is more hay to cut. A week passes with another postponement, a cutting for a neighbor. I keep my silence. I hope I am passing Jake Smucker's test.

Finally Jake calls to say that he can come to have a look at my spring house. Will I pick him up this afternoon? It has been two months since I asked. Over that time, I have worried more about our still anonymous connection than about my spring, which clearly needs attention. There is a crack in its tomblike enclosure—"Built by Amos Haas, 1932," the inscription on the enclosure reads—and the reservoir has lost some parging. Still, in this dry part of the summer, the haying time, water pours reassuringly through the moss-covered overflow. I know nothing about my spring. It is a mystery, like Jake Smucker, whom I fetch in my red Toyota. As I pull into the driveway at Jake's house, two older Amish women appear and as quickly disappear behind green blinds pulled down quickly from inside. Just as I decide to go to the door, Jake emerges. We shake hands, and Jake finally introduces himself by name, deliberately and formally.

"My name is Jake Smucker," he says. He offers me his identity along with his hand and looks fixedly into my eyes as he did that day at the sale. I return his gaze. If we suddenly have a bond of trust, I do not know why.

"My name is John Binns," I say. Jake's handshake is firm, unreserved and unguarded.

It is as if we meet for the first time. Jake is relaxed and welcoming, and I feel inhibited by his reordering that I do not understand. Immediately, he invites me in to show me the stone home that he has built. Although the masonry on the outside is fancy, inside the house is Amish plain, sparsely furnished and immaculately clean. From the kitchen, I hear quiet conversation and the clatter of crockery as the women prepare food, but we do not go there, and I do not see Emma or the children.

Outside, Jake invites me to inspect his ingenious stone spring run that provides running water for his house—pressurized indoor plumbing. We climb up stone steps laid into the hillside, just above the house, and Jake proudly shows me his spring, securely housed within its stone enclosure. From the overflow, water pours into a deep catch basin; at the bottom, an underground pipe directs water into the house. Jutting out from the steep slope, the catch basin overflows in a strong cascade into a stone watering trough for Jake's mules and horses. Jake has built around his water and protected its source. I remember an old Bible lithograph of Hagar and Ishmael's well in the desert. In this cool oasis, Jake's carriage horses stand by their elegant watering trough and switch flies with their tails in the afternoon heat, while an arrogant peacock marks his territory by uttering a shrill call over the peaceful sound of falling water.

For the site of his new home, Jake has selected a hidden dale with a clear view up the valley. His new house is off the road—close, yet remote. To the east, the white spire of Klinger's Lutheran Church, as diminutive as a crèche toy in the distant, green, rolling landscape, shimmers against an indigo sky. From Jake's farm, no other house can be seen except his daughter's, across the creek.

Jake removes the tethers from the horses and leads them to their stalls in the barn. The three boys I saw two months ago—without their hats, their hair is the color of cornsilk—emerge quietly but expectantly from the house and cluster around my red car.

"Would you like to come with us?" I ask. Jake nods his assent, and without a word, the boys immediately slip into the back seat in a silent, orderly, almost single motion.

We drive up the valley. As we pass the burial ground of Klinger's Church, Jake's stonecutter's eyes see tombstones, and farther down the road, bridge footers, culvert drains and the foundations of old barns. From the back seat, the three boys discuss road kill and ask Jake whether a now indistinct patch of flesh and fur is a skunk or a raccoon. Jake answers, *"Ein Rakoon, ein weiss-und-braun starbt Rakoon"* A raccoon, a white-and-brown dead raccoon.

Things are. Things happen.

Jake says we have had a "stalled introduction," and, as if to make up for it, he becomes quite talkative. He says he is "twice an immigrant." His people, Swiss Mennonites, came to Pennsylvania in the 1740s. Until four years ago, when he came north to find land that was "open and not so full of people," Lancaster County was Jake's home. He likes it here, just to the south of Mahantongo Mountain. It is a good place to raise the young boys. "It has been hard for Emma, as it was for Isaac, who never wanted to come up here and leave our father," Jake says, naming his half-brother. "Emma misses her large family in Lancaster County," he explains. "We have two houses in Lancaster County:

an old stone farmhouse and a large Victorian. My father lives there, in the big house. Yesterday my father visited here. He is now eighty-seven."

Jake's thoughts pull him away, and he looks out the car window. The boys discuss the route and decide they have not been on this road before. I stop the car at the top of Hooflander Mountain so they can look south, through the gap in Mahantongo Mountain, at Spread Eagle and see where they live. I tell the boys that on a clear day, you can see forty miles to the south, all the way to Lancaster County.

"That's where Isaac and Suzie went to live with our father." Jake names them both and looks toward the Lancaster Plain that lies beyond the gap. We get back into the car and Jake says, "I'm glad to be out of Lancaster County. *There*, it is not what you English think. Among us *here*, it is important to help each other."

Is he speaking of me or of other members of his Community? Outside his Community, I am *the other*. I am also *the English man*, who, Jake assumes, has an idyllic view of the Lancaster Amish. It is not true—it is beside the point—but I say nothing because what I hear is *here* and *there*, and I wonder why Isaac and Suzie first left *there*, Lancaster County, and now *here*. I wonder about Jake, too. Why did he leave an elderly father? Two houses? Two farms?

"You are lucky," I say, "to have family and live on the land close to your married daughter. I grew up on a farm. I've always been sorry I left, but now all my family is gone, there's no one to go back to. That's why I moved to Pennsylvania."

Jake smiles wanly; his blue eyes flash. I have said the wrong thing, and he becomes quiet. I want to erase this silence I have somehow created. Was it the mention of family? Nothing to go back to? Perhaps it was Luck—something that has nothing to do with Jake, who has made choices. He joined the Church, married into his Community, stayed on the land, and moved out of Lancaster County. Luck is an English, not an Amish, word. What did luck have to do with his half-brother's burned house? Jake's eyes darken, and I try to mend my mistake. *"Mehr Klug als Glück*—More wise than lucky."* I make a poor joke in bad German. I regret having said anything, especially in front of the boys, the oldest probably nine, the twins six or seven, all old enough to understand that the English man means well but, living outside their Amish world, does not think or say the right thing—cannot see or understand.

We pull into the driveway, and my dog runs out to greet the boys. We trail the boys, who follow the dog back through the meadow to the spring house. It is half past seven and still hot. We make small talk about the weather. Jake laughs to hear the English man's comments on the finer points of making hay. Today is a bright, magic day, probably the best day for haying of the whole year, so clear, hot and dry. As we walk up the creek bottom, the boys ask the name of every tree: shag-bark hickory, white oak, river birch, sour cherry, locust, walnut. I know the names; I could answer, but I am paralyzed by the boys' quiet manner, their overwhelming blond youth and innocence. I defer to Jake, who knows the names of the trees both in English and in his Pennsylvania-German dialect. Listening to him instruct the boys, I withdraw into my own thoughts. Why has he come? Is it trust? Is it no more than business? With thoughts like these tumbling in my head, I am afraid to name things—to exist in the world of things as they are.

"I'm glad you're here," I say. "I've worried about my spring since I discovered the crack this May, just after the fire. Perhaps the spring has shifted and I've lost my water. The old spring next to the house did that: it moved." Secure for over sixty years, a structure has failed, and foolishly, I believe this signifies something fundamentally wrong, a problem beyond mere mortar. It is my absurd thought, but there it is.

"Don't worry. I'll fix it. I understand springs—those things," Jake assures me.

The boys bob along the creek bank like little yellow ducks pursued by my black dog. We watch them play fetch with the dog, and Jake's eyes turn the deep, sparky blue they turned when I spoke of "luck" on the drive over. I am silent. I will not risk our tentative friendship by saying or wanting the wrong thing. Jake's being here this afternoon is important to me—and not just because of the spring house. I am the fool looking for grace.

My spring house is built into a bank. It is surrounded by ancient arbor vitae and white pine. Only with some difficulty do we pry open its rusted steel door, which gives way with a great groan. It has been twelve years since I last opened the spring house, and I wonder what secrets lie inside.

"The water looks good and full," Jake says, peering over the yellow heads of his three inquisitive boys. "I can fix the mortar. That will be easy, but I would not tamper with the spring. Springs, like people, are sensitive. You might lose your water."

Things are better than I remembered. The spring bubbles up gently through an ancient circle of set stones, and, like Jake's, its water runs through an underground pipe into a large reservoir. The race, formed by the overflow from the reservoir, is an orange-and-gold riot of jewel weed; the air around the spring is spicy from the fragile hay fern trampled by the curious boys, sharp from sweet nettle and water-cress. Quietly and industriously, the boys inspect the spring's environs.

"Has your spring ever run dry?" Jake asks.

"Not in the twelve years I've lived here," I reply.

"You are lucky," Jake says, repeating my word. "My oldest boy, who lives in the house we rebuilt—the house that burned—will come over next week to fix the mortar. You are fortunate to have a good spring. To have children and to be by good water is to be blessed in life." Is Jake quoting some source, or is this his own homily? After a moment, he asks, "How many children do you and your wife have?"

"We don't have any children," I reply. I do not explain because there is no reason; it is something that did not happen. Comfortable with silence, no longer needing to know, I won't ask how many children Jake has.

There is nothing more to say. Jake watches the boys peer into the spring house one last time. They gaze into the magic circle of stones surrounding the spring that has been pronounced fit by its magician, a better man than I to know its waters.

My dog decides it is time to go back to the house, and the boys tag along. Jake and I stay behind and listen to the sound of water pouring reassuringly out of the overflow. Time passes like a meditation. In the meadow, a breeze ripples the tall grass, and for a moment the boys' image stutters in the heat, like a mirage. Jake's eyes track the boys until only the tops of their heads are visible.

"Those boys aren't mine," Jake says. He speaks somewhat offhand-edly, but he stares straight on with his bright blue eyes, so like Isaac's, so like the eyes of the boys. "Those are Isaac and Suzie's.

"Suzie looks older than she is, I suppose. She thought she could never have children. She was over fifty when she had the first—the older boy—then the twins. Of course, she couldn't nurse, so Emma helped. Several women from our District Church helped her. When she had the twins, so late and not expecting them, she couldn't accept it. She asked Emma to take them. She said she didn't want them back. She laughed and said it wasn't God's grace but a joke. She became *verloss* —how do you English say?—lost, crazy. She tried to burn down the house with her and the boys in it. Not the house here, where they lived. There, in Lancaster County. We used to have three houses, my father, my family.

"Four years ago, Isaac agreed to let the farm go so Suzie could be near the boys. She didn't want them back, only to be closer. When she burned the house here, the boys were supposed to be at home with her, but it was Ascension Day and Isaac decided they'd go fishing.

"They don't know but that Emma's their mother. No one speaks of it."

Jake's eyes catch the blue solar flash of the sun as it drops below the horizon of the meadow, into a sea of flaming grass. The sun and the boys have disappeared.

William Richardson holds a Ph.D. in botany and plant physiology. This is his first published story.

Reviews

The Truth About Small Towns
by David Baker
University of Arkansas Press, 1998,
79 pp., $15 (paper)

"I don't want a song to make it all better/I don't want a home/to go home to," David Baker says in "Called Back," the first poem of this, his fifth book. In the thoughtful lyrics and understated narratives that follow, nothing does "make it all better," nor are we given the sense that the kind of small-town home Baker writes about can continue to exist except as Baker has preserved it for us in the fine language of this quiet collection.

These poems expertly make the rounds of small-town life. They speak of the fields, the trains, the "card shoppe," the movie theater's "blue velvet, dark aisles," the "new trees planted to beautify the block"—and, of course, the gossip so essential to parochial sensibility.

Throughout the book, but perhaps most acutely in the title poem, Baker is intent on documenting the passing of a well-loved way of life. The opening poem, which begins with the line "It never stops raining" and ends "It never rains," hints at the ambivalence

and contradiction Baker sees as typical of small towns. He navigates this world with moods ranging from the astringent to the sincere.

Baker's frustration with the inadequacy of language as a tool for preservation comes through substantially in several of the best poems. In "Top of the Stove," a narrative snapshot of a mother and child in a kitchen, the speaker observes, "Now they've gone. Language remains." The loss of the child's parents, pronounced in that single line, makes the persistence of words a cold comfort. "The Facts" tells of a deer crashing through a plateglass window. After the neighbors have gathered to see "the wild skin punctured . . . the brown leg pumping/a piston of want, muscle, bone," Baker writes, "we heard the train pull/away in the night,/and the animal/blood spread. Who knows why."

It's not only grief and violence that defy explanation in these poems but unreasoning tenderness as well. "The Kiss" conflates two camping trips, one from the speaker's childhood, one from the present moment, leaving him "waiting in the humming dark" for an unidentified someone "to kiss me once to sleep." Three love poems, "The Third Person," "The First Person," and "The Second Person," appear in that order, interspersed among the other pieces. Their common imagery of fire, smoke and sun provides a metaphor for all that burns bright and for all that burns out ,and it testifies to the elemental truth of life and loss. In these three carefully crafted poems—as in the others in David Baker's new book—we are reminded that our power to hold what we love is limited. (MB)

For Kings and Planets
by Ethan Canin
Random House, 1998, 335 pp., $24.95

Marshall Emerson is the gifted, charismatic but unsteady son of professor parents. Orno Tarcher, a self-proclaimed hayseed from Cook's Grange, Missouri, meets Marshall on his first day at Columbia University. The young men, who each view the other's world as exotic, become instant friends. Ethan Canin's new novel, For Kings and Planets, follows their turbulent relationship from college well into their professional careers as "O," the sturdy, reliable one, assumes the "chores of a tradesman" and becomes a small-town Maine dentist while "M," who aspires to write the great American novel, succeeds as a slick Hollywood producer instead.

The strength of the young men's friendship is challenged when Orno falls for Marshall's seemingly sweet, uncomplicated younger sister, Simone. The relationship gains him further entry into the academic family he

adulates. The Emerson/Pelham clan members are all charming and accomplished, but one senses that something sinister lurks beneath the sophisticated veneer. Like Dr. Emerson, with whom he's engaged in an ongoing battle, a "fight to the death," Marshall has an eidetic memory, a penchant for self-invention and a flair for violence. His mother, Mrs. Pelham, despite being a respected anthropologist, caters to her husband's needs and fails to protect her children from his often malevolent behavior. Orno loves Simone but is wary of joining a family whose seal, according to Marshall, is "a snake, twisted in knots."

Canin reminds us of the complexity and delicacy of friendship. Orno realizes that "he has been more disciple than friend" to Marshall and must learn to be less of a follower. Canin also writes about the pleasure of doing the unexpected, of the enjoyment of small things and of probing life's mysteries. He renders in exacting detail the architecture of New York City, the glitz of the Los Angeles landscape, and the placidity of small-town Maine life. His descriptions of rural Missouri, though, which include subzero temperatures, barren landscapes, and farmers with Scandinavian names, seem more like a stereotype of Minnesota or Wisconsin. Also, Canin's insistence on the deep-rooted differences between Midwesterners and Easterners may strike the reader as an artificial way of widening the gap between the two young men. But the captivating story of Orno and Marshall's friendship, along with Canin's elegant writing, sufficiently make up for these minor lapses. (KS)

You Are Not I: A Portrait of
Paul Bowles
by Millicent Dillon
University of California Press, 1998,
340 pp., $27.50

Paul Bowles occupies a unique place as an expatriot artist, partly because of the exoticism of his life and subject matter and partly because he composed both music and literature. Eighty-eight this year, he is internationally famous as an author through his novels, collections of short stories and nonfiction, and he continues to be well regarded as a composer, too.

Millicent Dillon first met Bowles in March of 1977, when she went to Tangier to gather information about his deceased wife, the writer Jane Bowles. The resulting biography, *A Little Original Sin: The Life and Work of Jane Bowles*, was published in 1981. Dillon continued to correspond with Bowles and in 1992 went again to Tangier to begin work on *You Are Not I* (a title borrowed from one of his stories).

The fact that fans, journalists and film crews had long since beaten a path to Bowles' door never completely dispelled the aura of secrecy around him, but Dillon's previous fifteen-year acquaintance with the author gave her a special entrée. In this portrait, she combines her conversations with Bowles with a perceptive narrative, and the result is an extremely alive and readable book.

A fascinating story it is. Born in 1910 on Long Island, Bowles evidenced a gift for composing and writing at an early age. In 1929 he abruptly left the United States for Europe without completing his fresh-man year at the University of Virginia. His departure marked the beginning of his life as an emigré, although he did return to the U.S. for short interludes. On the advice of Gertrude Stein, he traveled to Morocco for a time to study with Aaron Copland, and sixteen years later he returned to make Tangier his permanent home. He met Jane Auer in 1937, and when they married in 1938 they forged one of literature's most unusual alliances. With characteristic candor, Ms. Dillon writes that later in the same year the Bowleses began to "live separate sexual lives." Paul's work with Jane on the manuscript that became her novel *Two Serious Ladies* (published in 1943) inspired him to begin writing his own fiction again, and he embarked on the work that has now secured his reputation as a stylist and explorer of previously uncharted literary waters. Although Jane suffered a stroke in 1957 from which she never recovered physically or mentally, Paul remained devoted to her until her death in 1973.

After Jane's death, Paul temporarily stopped writing (he had finished his autobiography, *Without Stopping*, during her final illness). At one point he commented that after Jane was gone, he had "no one to write for." What comes through about his present life—in which physical discomfort, fatigue, and the demands of others are constants—is the portrait of a patient and courteous, if rather weary gentleman, unflamboyant yet charismatic. But finally, it's Dillon's ability to show us the workings of the younger, more fiery mind that created those intense and fabulous fictions that makes reading *You Are Not I* an adventure. (EK)

Confederates in the Attic—
Dispatches from the Unfinished
Civil War
by Tony Horwitz
Pantheon, 1998, 406 pp., $27.50

Spurred on by his own boyhood fascination with the Confederacy, Pulitzer Prize–winning journalist Tony Horwitz set off on an odyssey through Dixie to find explanations for America's continuing obsession with the Civil War. In *Confederates in the Attic*, he chronicles his adventure. In the process, he paints a sometimes amusing yet often sobering portrait of a region fixated on heritage and tradition, where the Confederacy and its ideals are sanctified by a surprising number of Southerners still in thrall to the legacy of the war. En route, Horwitz is awakened to the complexity of Southern identity, which appears deceptively simple to Northerners.

Horwitz introduces us to a host of unforgettable people and places. In Virginia, he encounters the weird subculture of hard-core Civil War reenactors, whose commitment to total authenticity produces a euphoric "period rush." In Kentucky he attends Klan rallies; in Alabama he meets Alberta Martin, the last living Confederate widow; in Andersonville he finds that the commander of the notorious prison there is now exalted as a martyr, his date of execution a local holiday; and in Richmond he encounters a heated civic debate caused by the city council's proposal to erect a memorial to Arthur Ashe alongside monuments of Confederate heroes. Along the way he visits cemeteries, battlefields and every conceivable sort of small-town shrine

dedicated to the Confederacy—for example, Jimmy Olger's folk museum, located on Robert E. Lee's retreat route to Appomattox, the main attraction of which is a life-sized, gold-spray-painted statue of Lee made from junk hardware and sheetrock. His visit to Olger's is part of the high point of his tour, a "Civil Wargasm" that consists of a seven-day pilgrimage to battlegrounds from Manassas to Gettysburg to Appomattox in the company of Robert Lee Hodge, an eccentric reenactor who prides himself on his authentic impression of a battlefield corpse.

In his quest for answers, Horwitz seeks out well-known historians such as Shelby Foote as well as countless homespun authorities who inform him that much of what he had learned about the war is more myth than fact. At the same time, he comes to realize how easily truth can be distorted and transformed to myth by local revisionists who conveniently reshape the past. The resulting "feel-good" history quickly becomes instilled in the native consciousness and is seldom refuted.

But beyond the larger-than-life characters and descriptions of peculiar locales is a very serious observation regarding the state of race relations in the U.S. Horwitz uncovers the deeply rooted antigovernment sentiment, bigotry and ignorance that lie just beneath the surface of the deceptively placid Southern landscape. His research brings him into contact with the flourishing network of neo-Confederate organizations, from the more well-known Southern institutions such as the Klan and the Sons of Confederate Veterans to the lesser-known Heritage Preservation

Association, with its toll-free hotline to report "heritage violations" whenever they occur.

Written with a combination of journalistic insight, humor and an eye for the bizarre, *Confederates in the Attic* brings to light a world that for many of us has heretofore remained well camouflaged behind the façade of our contemporary cultural homogeneity. Entertaining and picaresque, at times frightening and disturbing, this book is about more than just damn Yankees and the sanctity of the rebel flag. (BR)

Babylon in a Jar
by Andrew Hudgins
Houghton Mifflin, 1998, 72 pp., $22

The poems in Andrew Hudgins' fifth collection probe "the dead world's constant simmer," which to Hudgins' eye is everywhere apparent—on the nightly news, in his garden, at cocktail parties, in the classroom. His desire to recognize history's cycles of compounding violence and terror necessarily prevents the poet from settling into his daily comforts. *Babylon in a Jar* percolates with the dark intrusions of ruined empires, blood sacrifice and pain.

In "Poem," Hudgins catalogues the cities of the ages—Babylon and Nineveh, Athens, Berlin and Tenochtitlán—that come and go like the daffodils in the garden: "The murderous, back-/from-death pre-blossoming/blossoms, promising/the frilled afterthought/of flowers, bright cups/tipping in the March god's fist." Other poems lament contemporary society's loss of a sense of tragedy. In "Rain," as a serial killer terrorizes

Cincinnati, leaving female body parts to be found by the police, a woman student asks tentatively if the ancient myths the class is studying are no longer true. Hudgins thinks one thing and says another: "No,/it's not true anymore. We aren't all Isis./We won't all be Osiris." But, his own observations tell him as the poem concludes, "Like a small boy with a radio or frog,/we hack and reassemble our old unmurderable gods/so we won't tear each other into pieces./Eternity's a ball, history is a stick." Though such brutality cuts across the centuries and weighs on our daily negotiations, Hudgins says, "Let us/save outrage for our private lives."

Though Hudgins excels at the first-person, understated, anecdotal poem, one wishes at times for a more wrenching or ambitious syntax and diction to confront the mysteries that span the centuries. Hudgins' verse generally hinges on the state of mind of the speaker, asking the reader to buy into his plight, to believe what he says because he believes it. If Hudgins strives for something beyond the self, the poems should not depend so entirely on the self for access to it.

Testing the undergirding of the choices we make, individually and collectively, Hudgins' best poems locate a furious mystery in historical moments that have modern-day moral or political analogues. (PM)

Moby Dick, by Herman Melville (four-volume CD)
read by Bill Bailey
Naxos AudioBooks, 1998, 4 hrs. 43 min., $25.98, ISBN: 9626340266

The written word has in fact been spoken for most of its history. The Romans both composed and read their books orally. Cicero, for example, composed aloud by night, memorized his passages, then dictated them the next day to a scribe. In his fourth-century *Confessions*, St. Augustine recorded the first known description of someone reading silently and without moving his lips—the awesome scholar Ambrose. As late as the nineteenth century, when the most popular authors were also lecturers and readers, the oral presentation of texts remained as important as silent reading. Jane Austen read her compositions aloud to entertain family and friends. Most of the canonical authors of the nineteenth century were performers for private and public entertainment, and many of them read aloud to their friends for editing suggestions.

Certain books can best be experienced, or reexperienced, by listening to them. The growing variety of books on tape and CD provides great companions for travel, exercise or busy work. At *The Missouri Review*, we have decided to pick some of the best of these audio books for regular review.

What sets apart the four-volume CD of Herman Melville's 1851 novel *Moby Dick* (since this item can be somewhat hard to find, we have included the ISBN above) is the length of the recording—almost five hours—and the solid performance of the text. Melville's novel is full of high rhetoric and colorful vernacular, and Bill Bailey mercifully doesn't overdo it. For whole passages he reads almost quietly, nicely modulating Melville's word-intoxication.

As with many of the best quest tales, Captain Ahab's relentless pursuit of the giant albino whale can be read in many ways. Like a revenge play of the Elizabethan era, it tells of a monomaniacal pursuit by a powerful man caught in a recursive and shallow urge to avenge himself. Ahab is a gifted, intelligent man, made superficial by his inability to examine his own motives. He invests his enemy with metaphysical projections of evil or of transcendent meaning. Repeatedly Ahab must rally his forces to weld them to his purpose, lending political overtones to a tale that already has moral and metaphysical ones.

Though Ahab is a character who is hard to care about in the usual sense, his men are full of pathos and humanity, from the three colorful mates, Starbuck, Stubb and Flask, to the multicultural crew and the intelligent witness Ishmael, teller of the tale. The joy of this book is its largeness of purpose and its language, which is even more powerful to hear than to read. I will probably not reread *Moby Dick*, but I am now sure to listen to it again. (SM)

Prozac Diary
by Lauren Slater
Random House, 1998, 203 pp., $21.95

Though the story of a life lived on Prozac may sound like the stuff of talk shows, Lauren Slater's memoir, *Prozac Diary*, is a more analytical than confessional account of her ten-year experience with the drug. Slater, one of the first long-term users of Prozac, gives us a perspective that is unswayed by current prevailing stereotypes about its risks and benefits, imparting through her well-honed prose an experience that has been confusing, painful, and strangely beautiful.

Prozac Diary begins shortly after the FDA approved the use of Prozac in the late '80s, when a psychiatrist prescribed the medication to help treat Slater's obsessive-compulsive disorder and borderline personality disorder. She marveled at her quick reaction: "It was as though I'd been visited by a blind piano tuner . . . who had tweaked the ivory bones of my body, the taut strings in my skull, and now, when I pressed on myself the same notes but with a mellower, milder sound sprang out." Slater recounts how, in this transformation, she both gained and lost parts of herself, since the Prozac stifled her creativity along with her compulsive behavior. As she and Prozac continued their "growing up together" her feelings about this tradeoff became more and more ambivalent, until her Prozac "poop-out" on a research trip in Kentucky, which resulted in a relapse and a reevaluation of her relationship with the drug.

Slater effectively intertwines the story of her ongoing Prozac use with memories of her unstable childhood and psychologically disturbed mother. Though she has worked as a psychologist and holds an MA in psychology from Harvard, her account of her experience with Prozac could hardly be called clinical. Her memoir is striking for its humor, emotion and lucidity. She describes how she views her chemical "crutch" at times as a lover, at times as an adversary and in the end, as "a well-meaning buddy whose presence can considerably ease pain but cannot erase it." (JL)

Death in Summer
by William Trevor
Viking, 1998, 214 pp., $23.95

Following his best-selling novel, *Felicia's Journey*, and his fine short story collection, *After Rain*, the prolific Trevor's twelfth novel is an impeccably wrought small tragedy that illustrates how social class and circumstance are fate.

Thaddeus Davenant, whose privileged but curiously neglectful upbringing has left him eminently civilized but emotionally remote, has just lost his wife, Letitia, in a bicycle accident. When his mother-in-law, Mrs. Iveson, comes to help him interview prospective nannies for his infant daughter, Georgina, the two fail to find a suitable applicant, and Mrs. Iveson stays on to take care of the baby.

One of the applicants, Pettie, an unemployed orphan with forged references, is enchanted with Thaddeus' stately home, Quincunx House— a veritable palace in her eyes—and falls half in love with Thaddeus, who to her seems like a refined father figure. Pettie's only friend is the mildy retarded Albert, who was raised with her in the Morningstar Orphanage. Privately, Albert concurs with his landlady's description of Pettie as a lost soul, a "tearaway." Still, he helps feed and shelter her, out of loyalty and a profound, unswerving goodness that contrasts with Pettie's hard cynicism and makes him the moral center of this quietly allegorical book.

Crushed when she is turned down for the job at Quincunx House, Pettie returns there, ostensibly to look for a lost ring, scopes out the daily routine, and later kidnaps Georgina from the garden when Mrs. Iveson falls asleep while watching her. In the resulting panic and desperate search, Thaddeus finally grasps the significance of the relationships in his life: to Georgina, to Letitia, to Mrs. Iveson and to a former lover, an older woman, the now invalid Mrs. Ferry, whose subsequent death is the second of three referred to in the book's title. The third death, the tragic resolution, is not so much inevitable as perfectly justified and artfully staged.

Trevor is a master of his craft. It's no small feat to imbue a story with symbolic substance and moral heft while maintaining such an economy of characters, plot and pages. (ES)

The Professor and the Madman: A Tale of Murder, Insanity, and the Making of the Oxford English Dictionary
by Simon Winchester
HarperCollins, 1998, 242 pp., $22

This story of the birth of the *Oxford English Dictionary* traces the lives of two fascinating men: James Murray, who spent over forty years working on the first *OED* and still did not see it finished in his lifetime, and Dr. William C. Minor, an American Civil War veteran who spent much of his life incarcerated in the Broadmoor Criminal Lunatic Asylum in England. These two lives intersected through a practice, revived by Murray in the 1870s, of a lexicographer soliciting scholars for quotations to be used as references in the dictionary. Murray received more than 10,000 contributions from Minor over several years and for most of this time believed him to be a country doctor with a love of reading. Little did he know that Minor was in fact a condemned murderer and paranoiac sentenced to life imprisonment.

Winchester narrates the histories of both men, their eventual meeting upon Murray's investigation of Minor's absence from an *OED* dinner honoring contributors, and the friendship that survived the unveiling of Minor's criminal past. One of the most skillful facets of the book is the way these two men, each following vastly different paths, are shown to have been linked not only through the compilation of the *OED* but also through affinities in their personalities. Minor, a violent character renowned for excesses with drink and women, and Murray, a slightly pedantic, well-educated family man, would seem like complete opposites. Yet Winchester describes two men more similar than not, both of whom were crucial to the massive undertaking of the *OED*, which he describes as "a project that . . . was eventually to put James Murray on a collision course with a man whose interests and piety were curiously congruent with his own."

As interesting as the relationship between Minor and Murray is the story of how the *OED* came into being and the many obstacles it faced during the seventy years it took to complete it. The logistics of recording quotations that scholars such as Minor sent in are mind-boggling. Winchester so evidently enjoys describing this part of the project (which involved several employees and subeditors as well as a drafty shed and numerous shelves and pigeonholes) that the reader is swept up in a joyful contemplation of the trivia of the *OED*'s making. In fact, the delightful accounts of the day-to-day particulars of dictionary making almost overshadow the gory descriptions of Minor's murderous insanity and his Civil War traumas.

Winchester's tone is playful and self-consciously Victorian, as in his coyly euphemistic reference to the act of sexual intercourse as "the ultimate." More disturbing is his tendency to speculate, sometimes wildly. When relating Minor's arrival at the asylum, he writes, "He heard the outer gates open to let the carriage out, then close again. There was a resounding crash as the inner metal gates shut and were bolted and chained." Winchester's bent toward melodrama peaks in one of the last chapters of the book, where he proposes a lurid scenario in Minor's life, the unlikelihood of which even he seems ashamed by, since he brackets the scene with disclaimers describing it as "a reason that some might think rather stretches credulity" and "a possibility—not a probability to be sure." These forays into sensationalist fantasy detract from a story that is otherwise memorable for its wealth of detail. (TH)

Tomato Red
by Daniel Woodrell
Henry Holt & Company, 1998, 225 pp., $20

The unforgettable narrator of Daniel Woodrell's sixth novel is Sammy Barlach, a crank addict and surprisingly good natured loser in search of friendship. After a night in a drug-induced haze, Sammy breaks into a mansion in the little Ozark town of West Table, Missouri, intending to burglarize it. Instead, he falls asleep in a chair. He is awakened by Jamalee Merridew, a fiery redhead with delusions of grandeur, and her gorgeous brother, Jason. To satisfy Jamalee's yearning for the good life, the two routinely break into wealthy homes when the owners are away, dress in their clothes, eat their food and pretend to be rich people.

Out of loneliness, and the need to be someone's hero, Sammy soon becomes involved with Jamalee and her family, who live in Venus Holler, the poorest section of West Table. Bev, their mother, the town prostitute, has learned to endure, and even to enjoy, her miserable life, but Jamalee and Jason dream only of escape. Jamalee plans on using her "country queer" brother's extraordinary good looks to prostitute him to the wealthy female population of the town, then blackmail them to fund her extravagant dreams. The one thing that enables her to get through her miserable day-to-day existence is a vision of a better world in Beverly Hills.

Any of the vividly drawn main characters could lay claim to being the antihero of this book, but the novel really belongs to Sammy. Woodrell takes him on a journey through poverty, unexpected friendships—and even murder. With an ear for dialect and an eye for the details of "white trash" existence, the author creates memorable characters who, through their horrible naïveté, perform unbelievably stupid acts. Sometimes it is hard to know whether to root for them or slap them in the face.

In this fast-paced read there are so many plot twists that we never really know what is around the next corner (the last fifty pages alone could sell the book). But Woodrell's ability to turn a phrase is enthralling, and the roller coaster ride is so enjoyable that it finally doesn't matter where we end up. (JB)

Reviews by: Marta Boswell, Kris Somerville, Elizabeth Knies, Brett Rogers, Preston Merchant, Speer Morgan, Joy Luz, Evelyn Somers, Tina Hall, Jackie Bledsoe

---

American First Novels, 1998
by Bruce Allen

Nineteen ninety-seven was pretty much dominated by eagerly awaited and loudly trumpeted new works from many of America's most highly regarded novelists. Thomas Pynchon's imposing *Mason & Dixon* and Don De Lillo's encyclopedic *Underworld* topped most critics' polls, with works by such similarly grave and revered figures as Saul Bellow, Norman Mailer, Philip Roth and Louis Auchincloss lurking close behind them.

Nevertheless, that year's most honored fiction was Charles Frazier's richly detailed and deeply moving first novel, *Cold Mountain*, perhaps the finest portrayal to date in our literature of the Civil War and its effect on ordinary people.

If nothing of quite that stature has emerged from 1998's numerous debut novels, the year just past was nevertheless distinguished by at least a dozen vivid and interesting performances by new writers from whom we may surely expect even better things in the future.

A sad exception is the late Norma Peterson, whose posthumously published *Rhonda the Rubber Woman* **(Permanent Press, 247 pp., $24)** offers a feisty and endearingly funny portrayal of Nancy Sayers, who grows up in the small Pennsylvania town of Maryville in the 1930s–'40s under a cloud of disapproval seeded by the roundheeled lifestyle of her promiscuous mother, Georgia.

It's a coming-of-age tale made fresh by Peterson's invention of a resonant specific situation: Nancy, who's double-jointed, rises beyond notoriety and unpopularity when she performs as "Rhonda the Rubber Woman" in a two-bit traveling carnival. Peterson makes us believe that this tacky leap into modest celebrity is indeed a liberation—and that Nancy's journey to Philadelphia, where she seeks the truth about the father she's never known, is her triumph. One finishes this novel wanting to learn more about its splendid heroine, and regretful that Norma Peterson will not be able to continue her story.

Another very affecting picture of family and small-town life emerges in journalist Frederick Reiken's *The Odd Sea* **(Harcourt Brace, 224 pp., $22)**, which is set in the rural "hilltowns" of western Massachusetts and narrated by young Philip Shumway. It's a remembrance of Philip's thirteenth summer, when his much-loved older brother, Ethan, unaccountably disappeared and never returned. Reiken depicts the Shumways as a close, mutually supportive clan whose devastation over the loss of the boy who seemed the best of them all—Ethan was a precocious musician and composer—gradually and painfully unravels the fabric of accomplishment and content in which they've coexisted.

The novel's plot is imperfectly worked out: we don't know, and aren't sure whether we need to know, if Ethan was—as is strongly suggested—sexually molested and murdered, or if he simply walked away from a difficult relationship with an older woman who had been his mentor. But the great strength of *The Odd Sea* is its quiet, meditative focus on the emotional aftershock of Ethan's departure. Both his sister Amy's surging anger and the sorrowful transformations through which their father wills himself are believable and gripping. Paradoxically, the loss of his brother gives impetus to Philip, the fledgling writer, who laboriously composes "sketches in which [Ethan] magically came home," sustained by his conviction that "we owe it to the people we love to actually remember them when they're gone." This is a beautiful story.

The characters' actions and their consequences are more fully revealed in Michael Knight's virtuoso tale of adultery and murder, *Divining Rod* **(Dutton, 208 pp., $23.95)**, which appeared as half of a dual debut also including Knight's short-story collection, *Dogfight*. The story begins in the town of Sherman, Alabama, with sixty-three-year-old high school history teacher Sam Holladay's apparently unmotivated shooting of his neighbor, young attorney Simon Bell.

Then it backtracks, in gracefully counterpointed narratives spoken by its several major characters, to explore the affair between Simon and Sam's much younger wife, Delia, as well as the Holladays' improbable though truly loving marriage. Knight's story comprehends, too, the lives of the Holladays' variously involved and affected family and neighbors (the most vivid among the latter is the "mad" Betty Fowler, whose wanderings with a dowsing rod "divining for gold" parallel the principal characters' compromised searches for fulfillment through romantic love).

From a story that could easily have veered into melodrama, Knight fashions instead a convincingly dispassionate composite portrait of lives unhappily thrown together. He tells us so much about Simon's, Sam's, and Delia's separate and shared pasts that we understand the experience that burdens and shapes them—and we feel real sympathy for them all. Delia wants desperately to love both men but knows she cannot. Sam's response is a painfully credible mixture of outrage and resigned acceptance. And Simon's fascination with the beautiful Delia, which he attributes to "an excess of capacity in the heart," seems both patently selfish and understandable—the effect of a charm he's powerless to resist.

Divining Rod very nearly sucumbs to overplotting in its later chapters, following Sam's arrest and imprisonment, but Knight rescues it with a visionary final scene that caps off, with cinematic intensity, this rhetorically sophisticated and highly visual work of fiction. First-timer Michael Knight is already a very accomplished writer.

In *The Treatment* (Knopf, 269 pp., $23), veteran short story writer and former *New Yorker* editor Daniel Menaker focuses more benignly on the amusingly addled psyche of Jake Singer, a prep school English teacher whose early midlife crisis—if, in fact, it is such—consists of unresolved relationships with the gorgeous women who keep entering his life and emotional combat with his psychiatrist, Dr. Ernesto Morales, a tyrannical comic monster whom Philip Roth might have dreamed up.

Jake is an appealing character, as are his former girlfriend Samira ("a gift from sex heaven") and current love interest, Allegra, a handsome widow. The only false note in this elegant, entertaining comedy is Jake's unconvincingly full understanding of his own shortcomings and defenses; if he knows himself this thoroughly, we wonder, why bother with Dr. Morales? But Menaker ends the novel with a wry and subtle point of indeterminacy, persuading us that in the last analysis, whether or not he breaks free from Morales's smug stranglehold, Jake Singer will keep on muddling endearingly through.

Allegra Goodman's *Kaaterskill Falls* (Dial, 324 pp., $23.95), which follows her highly praised story collections *Total Immersion* and *The Family Markowitz*, deftly portrays the complex interactions among a group of New York Jewish families, both at home in Washington Heights and during three summers in the late 1970s at the upstate vacation resort town where their social and religious solidarity and integrity are tested.

With the exception of a few minor characters who really don't belong in the story and a labored subplot about an anti-Semitic judge, the novel works beautifully. It's a moving dramatization of the clash between traditional values and the individual urge toward independent thought.

That conflict is embodied in the families of Andras Melish, who escaped Europe prior to the Holocaust and has built around himself a wall of sardonic disengagement from American Jewry's passionate bond with the old countries; "Rav" (Rabbi) Elijah Kirshner, a devout scholar burdened by the spiritual legacy he must pass on to one of two sons who are both as different from him as can be imagined; and especially English-born Elizabeth Shulman, a devoted and dutiful mother of five, whose romantic yearnings to make something more of herself force her into disagreement with her husband, Isaac's (and their culture's), firm admonition, "You have to want what you have."

Though these tensions are never completely resolved, Goodman infuses her quietly harrowing tale with considerable drama and brings it to a muted conclusion that's both credible and ineffably sad. She does not scruple to demonstrate that the supportiveness of the group is purchased at the cost of its members' individual energies and essential freedom. The "long pious shadows of the men walking to shul" cast themselves wide and far, and darken at least as much as they illuminate.

Danzy Senna's wonderfully titled *Caucasia* (Riverhead, 353 pp., $24.95) also tells a story of painful detachment from one's roots. Its likable protagonist and narrator is Birdie Lee, the light-skinned second child of a racially mixed couple whose strained marriage ends, sending her black father, Deck, and darker-skinned sister, Cole, abroad in search of racial harmony and contentment, while Birdie "passes" easily as white, along with her mother, Sandy, who reinvents them both as widowed Sheila Goldman and daughter Jesse.

Senna, who is herself of mixed race, makes Birdie's "state of incompletion" achingly real while also painting wonderfully replete pictures of the 1970s civil rights movement in the Northeast and of the quasi-Nabokovian small-town America through which "Sheila" and "Jesse" pass. This very good novel has understandably been compared to Mona Simpson's mother-and-daughter road novel, *Anywhere But Here*, but it also reminded me of the education experienced by the plucky kids of *To Kill a Mockingbird*.

The call of blood is louder still in Phyllis Alesia Perry's stark *Stigmata* (Hyperion, 240 pp., $21.95), whose central character, a black woman named Elizabeth ("Lizzie") Dubose, painfully lives the truth of her great-aunt Eva's simple homily: "The past ain't never really gone, is it?"

As her strange story begins, thirty-four-year-old Lizzie is being released from the most recent of the several "nuthouses" in which she has been confined for a history of repeated suicide attempts and self-mutilations. But the marks on Lizzie's wrists and legs seem to have been made by chains, like those worn by slaves—and, in a beautifully paced

series of searing disclosures, we learn that her "madness" has in fact been her experience of possession by the ancestors whose ordeals she helplessly recapitulates.

The stories of Lizzie's grandmother Grace (reviled as an "infamous woman" who abandoned her husband and children) and of their ancestor Bessie, whose African name was Ayo and who came to America on a slave ship, gradually and powerfully emerge from a complex mosaic narrative emblemized by the quilt Grace leaves to Lizzie and dominated by such masterly moments as Lizzie's dreamlike sighting of the long-dead Ayo standing in a cornfield leaning on a hoe.

A subplot involves Lizzie's playful and gratifying romantic relationship with a compassionate lover, but though it is sweet and entirely credible, this love affair seems a far less substantial kind of healing than Lizzie's tortured plunge into the world of her mothers. In its best moments—and there are many of them—*Stigmata* is a deeply felt and accomplished book.

Another debut novel, notable, by contrast, for its very winning rendering of what its author calls a "world of decency and kindness, goodness and laughter" is Van Reid's enjoyably faux-Dickensian *Cordelia Underwood; or, The Marvelous Beginnings of the Moosepath League* (Viking, 400 pp., $24.95). This first volume of a promised trilogy originally appeared serially in Maine's *Lincoln Weekly*. It's an episodic, comic romance written in direct imitation of that masterpiece of calculated formlessness, *The Pickwick Papers*.

Reid's amusingly intricate tale, set in late-nineteenth-century coastal Maine, features pirates and a mysterious legacy; tame bears and somewhat wilder human performers, including a lissome lady balloonist; the eponymous feisty heroine; and a manly young swain fetchingly named Sundry Moss. There's also a trio of ingenuous comrades whose misadventures compose the origins of the Moosepath League of the title. The story's convivial protagonist, portly, middle-aged Tobias Walton, possesses the Dickensian quality of somehow being on the scene whenever the unfortunate require his largesse or the villainous scheme to test his mettle. Nobody will much believe any of the high-spirited nonsense Van Reid puts his characters through, nor will anybody much mind the happy incredulity of it all.

An equally unconventional novelistic debut was made by short-story writer G.W. Hawkes (*Playing Out of the Deep Woods*), who published two full-length novels in successive months last year. *Surveyor* (**MacMurray & Beck, 200 pp., $20**) is the story of two Korean War veterans, John Suope and Paul Merline, Hawkes's narrator, whose postwar friendship took them, thirty years earlier, to the New Mexico desert and jobs as surveyors mapping remote areas for a mysterious "Foundation," the purposes of which they would never learn.

That scarcely matters, and, to be truthful, only minimally interests the reader. Hawkes' real subject is the edgy, unusual symbiosis in which the two men exist, amid "visions of wagon trains and cattle cars of dirty, happy families pouring in and raising a community"; the patently metaphorical presence of a young woman who erects an elaborate structure in an area vulnerable to floods in order to film its certain destruction for her Ph.D. dissertation; and the depredations of "dinosaur men" on an archaeological dig that simply begs to be subverted. It sounds rather like a reprise of Edward Abbey's *The Monkey Wrench Gang*, but Hawkes' novel reveals an original mind at work. He renders his oddball antiheroes' ornery insularity in crisp, sensuous prose, alert to minuscule details of landscape, weather and interior emotional shifts. It's a small story that keeps on resonating long after you've finished it.

Its companion publication, *Semaphore* (**MacMurray & Beck, 175 pp., $17**), treads even stranger ground: the inmost thoughts of its protagonist, Joseph Taft. Joseph has been mute for no discernible physical reason since birth. In a lyrical narrative distinguished by gorgeous atmospheric descriptions ("the warm rush of summer air vibrating with the wings of insects and the perfumes of growth and decay"), Hawkes renders with great intensity the eerie extent of Joseph's distance from others. He can foresee—in fact, virtually *experience*—random future events, such as the death of his young sister in a neighbor's swimming pool (which, to the consternation of his outraged parents, Joseph pathetically attempts to destroy).

Bridges are gradually built between Joseph and the world that cannot understand him, and he grows into manhood and marriage finally reconciled to his complex singularity, and to the burdens imposed by his "gift"—which is wonderfully encapsulated in the novel's valedictory conclusion, Joseph's unspoken blessing directed to trick-or-treating children impatient to break away from their protective parents: "Go, I love you, Come back, Take care, Goodbye. Go on."

The Iraqui assault on Kurdistan and the Spanish Civil War are prominent theaters of conflict in *Triage* (**Scribner, 240 pp., $23**), by Scott Anderson, a journalist best known for his scorching *Harper's Magazine* article, "Prisoner of War," about the holocaust in Bosnia. In the nightmarish opening scene, war photographer Mark Walsh awakens to find himself wounded, in a Kurdish field hospital. Walsh returns home to New York City, leaving behind his colleague and friend Colin, to repair his exhausted body and spirit with the aid of his Spanish-born lover, Elena.

A somewhat contrived coincidence brings onto that scene Elena's grandfather Joaquín Morales, a psychiatrist formerly known as "the Fascist Father Confessor," who had helped rehabilitate emotionally shattered members of Franco's murderous "blood squads." A tense nexus of interrelationships develops among the traumatized Mark, the egoist Joaquín and the unforgiving Elena. The two men each learn to face what is buried in their pasts, and, as they do, this often overpowering novel reveals the paradoxical truth at its core: that "it was a terrible thing to be the one who lived, who survived . . . this could be a weight in your heart that never left."

Colson Whitehead's *The Intuitionist* (**Anchor, 255 pp., $19.95**), a novel patently inspired by Ralph Ellison, explores with trenchant wit the dangerous world of its protagonist, young black elevator inspector Lila Mae Watson. She's the first female so employed in the "famous city," presumably a future New York. When a case of "total freefall" occurs in one of her elevators, it prompts official scrutiny of Lila's perfect safety record and sends her on an investigation to clear herself of wrongdoing.

Whitehead's delicious plot turns on the political battle for control of the Department of Elevators between Empiricists, who seek out literal physical causes of material wear and mechanical failure, and Intuitionists like Lila, who, through meditation, simply "sense" where and when an elevator will fail. Lila's quest to restore her reputation brings her into contact with helpful reality instructors and devious opportunists alike. The novel climaxes with her inconclusive discoveries about the life and mission of Intuitionism's founder, James Fulton, who was/is (it's uncertain whether he's still alive) either a visionary committed to improving the quality of urban life or a trickster who has manipulated to his advantage the truism that "white people's reality is built on what things appear to be."

The Intuitionist succeeds on all its several levels: unconventional mystery tale; the heroine's journey in search of knowledge; bracing satire; and allegory of racial inequality and struggle. A brilliant book.

There's also a formidable intelligence at work in Martha Cooley's *The Archivist* (**Little, Brown, 328 pp., $22.95**), an intricately layered story in which the world of literary scholarship is shown to conceal complex and unresolved passions. Its teasing opening section is set in "one of America's most prestigious institutions of higher learning," where a library archivist, Matthias, a sixtyish widower, tends a special collection whose prize exhibit is a series of letters from T.S. Eliot to a young American woman, Emily Lane, for whom he had hoped to leave his unstable wife, Vivienne. That the latter soon died and Eliot never did pursue a relationship with Emily are facts of consuming interest to Roberta Spire. Roberta, an ambitious graduate student, finds in Eliot's retreat into Catholicism a troubling analogue to her own parents' apostasy (they have converted from Judaism to Christianity).

Roberta's persistence "unseals" both the Eliot collection and Matthias' buried memories of his late wife Judith. When Cooley shifts from Matthias' embattled solitude to the near hysteria expressed in Judith's diary, the effect is instant and electric: the theme of emotion's unruly reality, despite our efforts to manage or suppress it, is vigorously dramatized. That's the real achievement of *The Archivist*: a knowing portrayal of the intellectual life that incisively elaborates both its rewards and its limitations.

Finally, to the best first novel I read last year. C.S. Godshalk's thrilling *Kalimantaan* **(Marian Wood/Holt, 472 pp., $25)** is a rich historical romance about the early-nineteenth-century conquest of Sarawak, a part of Borneo formerly known as Kalimantaan.

The man who both ravishes and is ravished by this pristine, violent, near primitive land is Gideon Barr, an egotist who would be king and who is supported by a British government eager to open new trade routes to the East.

Godshalk's characterization of Barr as faintly absurd, driven less by his lust for power than by a desire to be worthy of his late mother's approval, undercuts the self-glorifying myth of the white man's burden—as do several other superb inventions. Among them are the resourceful independence demonstrated by the native Dyak tribes, the brutal acquisitiveness indulged in by Barr's nephew and successor, Richard Hogg (a character Robert Louis Stevenson might have conceived), and especially the conciousness that grows in Barr's young bride, Amelia, another of his "possessions," whose compassionate identification with the culture they have appropriated and traduced raises her above her husband and changes her life.

Brief summary can only suggest the richness of *Kalimantaan*: a brilliant pageant that brings to life an alien place and way of life; a thoughtful critique of imperialism and colonialism; and, best of all, a compulsively readable story of memorable characters placed in fateful interrelationship. C.S. Godshalk's is the most assured and eloquent among the many new novelistic voices first heard in 1998. She is presently at work on her second book, "a contemporary novel set in New England." Whatever worlds this writer subsequently explores will be places well worth visiting.

ARDENTIA UNDERGRADUATE
AWARD IN LITERATURE

Win $100 for 1st place in poetry and fiction
and get published in
Ardentia Art and Literary Magazine

$25 and publication
for runner up in each category

Deadline is September 1, 1999
Open to all undergraduates at all colleges and universities.
$10 entry fee includes 1 year subscription.

Send submissions to:
A022 Brady Commons
University of Missouri-Columbia
Columbia, MO 65211
or call (573) 882-1803

*No more than ten poems may be submitted per person.
Fiction may be no more than 5,000 words.*

෧෬

ANNOUNCING THE NEW

Mid-American Review

Sherwood Anderson Fiction Award
&
James Wright Poetry Award

1st Prize, Each Genre: $300 & Publication.

2nd through 5th Place: notation in prize-winning issue, plus possible publication.

1999 JUDGES

Fiction: June Spence
author of
Missing Women and Others

Poetry: Scott Cairns
author of
Recovered Body and
Figures for the Ghost

Deadline Extended to June 15, 1999! $10 entry fee (check or money order, made out to *Mid-American Review*) for each story (5,000 words or less) or each set of three poems. Submissions will not be returned. Entries should not be under consideration elsewhere. All participants will receive a copy of *Mid-American Review*, Volume XX, the twentieth anniversary double issue, where the winners will be published. Send entries to:

Mid-American Review
Attn: 1999 Sherwood Anderson / James Wright Competition
Department of English
Bowling Green State University
Bowling Green, Ohio 43403

the Green Hills
LITERARY LANTERN

Featuring

Dennis Saleh
Sofia M. Starnes
B. Z. Niditch
Simon Perchik
Donald Levering
Gayle Elen Harvey

Ted D. Barber
Dika Lam
Seteney Shami
Scott Jones
James Longstaff
Bruce Tallerman

Recent Contributors

Jim Thomas
Mary Winters
Chris Dungey
R. Nikolas Macioci
Nancy Cherry
David Wright

Walter Cummins
Doug Rennie
Geoffrey Clark
Ian MacMillan
Leslie Pietrzyk
Robert C. S. Downs

*Current Issue
Available Now, Price $7.00*

Send Orders to:
**the Green Hills
Literary Lantern
P.O. Box 375
Trenton, MO 64683**

Or Order by e-mail:
jksmith@netins.net

Published at:
North Central Missouri College

*Financial assistance for this project
has been provided
by the Missouri Arts
Council, a state agency.*

ekeppel

the modern writer as witness

Special Issue
American Families

WITNESS

Volume XII Number 2 $7   1998

Contributors

Marcia Aldrich
Pete Fromm
Dan Gerber
Jean Ross Justice
Julia Kasdorf
Anna Keesey
Maxine Kumin
Thomas Lynch
Joseph McElroy
Roland Merullo
Kent Nelson
Linda Pastan
Maureen Seaton
Floyd Skloot
Paul West

"From its inception, the vision that distinguishes Witness *has been consistent: it is a magazine situated at the intersection of ideas and passions, a magazine energized by the intellect, yet one in which thought is never presented as abstraction, but rather as life blood. Each issue is beautifully produced and eminently readable."*

Stuart Dybek

Call for Manuscripts:

Witness invites submission of memoirs, essays, fiction, poetry and artwork for a special 1999 issue on **Love in America.**
Deadline: July 15, 1999.

Writings from *Witness* have been selected for inclusion in *Best American Essays, Best American Poetry, Prize Stories: The O. Henry Awards,* and *The Pushcart Prizes.*

Oakland Community College
Orchard Ridge Campus
27055 Orchard Lake Road
Farmington Hills, MI 48334

Individuals
1 year / 2 issues $15
2 years / 4 issues $28

Institutions
1 year / 2 issues $22
2 years / 4 issues $38

Many Mountains Moving

Many Mountains Moving: a literary journal of diverse contemporary voices celebrates the richness of human diversity and life through literature and art. We showcase work from internationally renowned authors such as Sherman Alexie, Robert Bly, Lorna Dee Cervantes, Allen Ginsberg, Diane Glancy, Ursula K. Le Guin, Marge Piercy, Adrienne Rich, and Luis Urrea, and open our pages to outstanding new talents. We introduce our readers to people and cultures they might not otherwise visit, from voices with a unique perspective about the world—voices such as Charen, a Sri Lankan Tamil poet whose moving poetry has placed him at risk from both his government and Tamil separatist militant groups, and Rita Kiefer, an ex-nun improvising hymns to the geometry of her body.

Cover art by John Lucas

literature by women